Date Due

D

Fielding's Art of Fiction

Fielding's Art of Fiction

ELEVEN ESSAYS ON

Shamela, *Joseph Andrews*, *Tom Jones*, and *Amelia*

by

Maurice Johnson

Philadelphia
University of Pennsylvania Press

Prefatory Note

Publications of some twentieth-century commentators, especially Cross, Digeon, de Castro, Woods, and Sherburn, allow me to make assumptions that no longer require belaboring:

(1) *Shamela* was unquestionably Henry Fielding's work, and as his first, least-known, and least available fiction it deserves full explication; (2) the structure of *Joseph Andrews* needs no apology but perhaps enforces the theme of the book; (3) *Tom Jones's* "perfect plot" is a matter of control over all the elements of fiction, not of merely mechanical symmetry; and (4) *Amelia* shows that Fielding had not "gone soft" but that he used tough artistry to achieve success with his most challenging problems of construction and theme.

After writing tentatively on *A Journey from this World to the Next* and the incomparably superior *Jonathan Wild,* I have decided not to include essays on those works in this study of Fielding. They lie outside the direct progression from *Shamela* to *Joseph Andrews* to the achievement of *Tom Jones* and *Amelia,* in which I am more interested.

My quotations from Fielding's fiction are taken from the following sources, all in the University of Pennsylvania Library unless otherwise noted: *Shamela,* facsimile of " 2nd " ed., 1741, ed. Ian Watt, Augustan Reprint Soc. Publ. No. 57 (Los Angeles, 1956), compared with 1st ed., Rosenbach Museum, Philadelphia; *Joseph Andrews,* text based on 2nd ed., 1742, ed. J. Paul de Castro (London, 1929), compared with 1st and 3rd eds.; *Tom Jones,* "2nd" ed., 1749 (Mary Lepell Hervey's copy), compared with "3rd" ed. used as basis for text in Shakespeare Head Ed. (Oxford, 1926); *Amelia,* 1st ed., 1751 (dated "1752"), compared with text in Arthur Murphy's ed. of *Works,* 2nd ed., 1762.

I am grateful to James L. Clifford and Arthur H. Scouten,

who dropped their own work to read my manuscript and voiced their objections, some of which I have tried to satisfy through revising. In altering the arrangement of material or the language here and there, I have followed the suggestions of Sheridan Baker, Earl R. Wasserman, and William E. Miller.

Under the title of "The Device of Sophia's Muff in *Tom Jones*," and in somewhat different form, a portion of Chapter VIII has been published in *Modern Language Notes*.

This book is for Scott Dilworth Johnson, to read when he has read through Fielding's fiction once.

M.J.

Contents

Fielding's Art of Fiction

Introduction

These essays are meant for readers who are interested in Henry Fielding's fiction, not so much in its historical or biographical context, as in terms of art (and comic artifice). Except for one essay on literary theory in *Tom Jones,* my approach is through a series of separate explications, interpreting structural effects or analyzing specific passages.

If meaningful explication of poetry is rigorous and risky, it is even more so for long prose fiction. There is danger of never pushing very far beyond mere paraphrase or random verbal excavations. Because this " close " approach to Fielding's works, in order to be effective, must try to demonstrate that what appears to be a jungle of details is in reality an artfully planted garden, it is a more exacting approach (for explicator and reader alike) than the easy-sounding, general, appreciative evaluations which leave the text itself almost out of account. But such generalizations, after being enjoyed and agreed with, seem to me to have the vexing habit of evaporating when consulted for proof of accomplishment in fiction. I have tried to display the evidence. Although I deal with the works in chronological order and do, I hope, illustrate the growth and refinement of Fielding's art, my essays need not be read consecutively : readers may wish to begin with the novels they know best.

I had better say here, at the outset, that by " explication " I do not mean the ingenious deciphering of private codes in Fielding's fiction. If he left any willfully unresolved obscurities, I am not aware of them. Through some close scrutiny of his works, I do intend to show that, although he dwelt on the ambiguities of human nature and of Fortune, Fielding rendered those ambiguities in prose which, at its best, reached the ideal of perfect aptness and accessibility.

Henry Fielding's mind, as it shows itself in his fiction, reflects his activity as a man. Contemplative and vigorous, theoretical and practical, making and judging, he excelled in the two worlds of fiction and life; but he excelled most lastingly in his entertaining amalgamation of those worlds.

To try to convey the impression of real experience in his fiction, and to " laugh Mankind out of their favourite Follies and Vices," he sometimes worked through parody, irony, and wit, tricking and shocking his reader, dissimulating and feigning. That is to say, he was an artist.

What any artist puts down on paper is of course artifice, ordered and selective as experience never is. By means of his artifice the writer labors to create the effect of an actual world inhabited by real people, more comprehensibly lifelike than our chaotic, fleeting impressions outside his fiction. In this effort he may audaciously point out to us his illusionary apparatus, deliberately letting us glimpse the workings of his shadow-boxes and cardboard properties. He may surprise us into awareness by means of incongruities, outrageous parallels, *trompe-l'oeil* devices, self-conscious conversations with " the reader," plays within plays, stories within stories, interpolated fables : against its black velvet backdrop the apparatus of illusion is meant to dispel and transcend illusion. " But literary artifice is the only means that a writer has at his disposal," says Harry Levin. " How else can he convey his impression of life? Precisely by discrediting those means, by repudiating that air of bookishness in which any book is inevitably wrapped." [1]

Ambiguities in Fielding's fiction are "intentionally tantalizing." I borrow the phrase from George Sherburn, who goes on to say that Fielding "frequently plays his reader as a fisherman might a

---

[1] Harry Levin, " The Example of Cervantes," *Society and Self in the Novel: English Institute Essays, 1955,* ed. Mark Schorer (New York, 1956), p. 6.

trout."[2] The delighted reader allows himself to be hooked and led through a series of reversals, discoveries, reappearances, and involvements of character and plot. With equal delight the reader allows himself to be captured in traps of verbal irony, sometimes encountering one trap hidden inside another, baited with inno- cent-sounding words like "great," "good-natured," "prudent," and "passions." Occasionally the intention seems to be that of testing the reader's powers of discrimination, as Jane Austen later delighted to do. Fielding tests his reader into thought, for instance, by his somewhat ambiguous handling of the final rela- tionships of Joseph and Parson Adams and of Tom and Squire Allworthy.

When he leaves Greek and Latin untranslated, in what seem to be significant contexts, he tantalizes the unschooled reader; and when he provides a humorously distorted translation, he pushes his test further. For the schooled reader will not only be able to share the joke of intentional mistranslation but can laugh at the innocent confusion of his unsuspecting fellows. Thus, to some extent, the work of fiction is not only *about* experience, but may *become* the experience. The reader, though he may at first balk and kick against it, finds himself altered into one of the fictitious characters.

André Gide, seeking complete possession of human experience in the novel form, deliberately interwove and contrasted the elusiveness of reality and the logic of fiction in *The Counter- feiters*. As he described in " Notes en Manièr de Préface à *Tom Jones*," Gide thought a twentieth-century novelist could profit from study of Fielding's devices, especially that of the intrusive author, the " Henry Fielding " of the prefaces and interrupting commentaries.

In all fiction worth rereading, even in *Moll Flanders* and *Madame Bovary,* which are supposed to be triumphs of "author-

---

[2] George Sherburn, " A Novelist's Opinions and His Art," *Sewanee Review,* LXI (Spring, 1953), 320.

lessness," we sense — through the artifice — the distinctive image of
an author who has projected himself into his work, taken us into
his confidence, and defined himself in his handling of the various
fictional modes of truth. Fielding's self-conscious " authorship "
is intentional artifice, one of the identities he assumed for publication of his works. At one time or another he was H. Scriblerus
Secundus, Captain Hercules Vinegar, Mr. Conny Keyber, Petrus
Gualterus, John Trottplaid, Esq., and Sir Alexander Drawcansir.
When, as " Henry Fielding," he rudely breaks into his fictional
world with an anecdote of his own, or when he suddenly exchanges his straightforward, colloquial manner for the mock-
heroic vein, he reminds the reader of the interplay of reality and
illusion. Like Cervantes he hopes to effect a flashing compre-
hension of truth through shifting perspectives, metamorphoses,
and parody.

And it was something of this kind that interested Gide in
Fielding's fiction. " For Gide," W. B. Coley writes, " the ideal
work of art must contain within it a paradigm or parody of
itself. Properly devised, such a parody will appear to resolve the
rivalry between the real world and the representation art makes
of it in favor of the artistic representation. The effect is achieved
by heightening the superlative and minute artifice of the parody,
so that what surrounds it, the bulk of the total work, seems ' real '
by comparison."[3]

Fielding not only dramatized and parodied the ambiguous
relationship of experience and fiction, but he more than once
commented on that relationship in his prefaces. In his final work,
published posthumously, he remarked that the great, original
poets are not "so properly said to turn reality into fiction, as
fiction into reality" (Preface, *Voyage to Lisbon*). He was much
aware of Aristotle's analysis of the function of the artist, who
works in a world of semblances and imitates things not as they

---

[3] W. B. Coley, " Gide and Fielding," *Comparative Literature*, XI (Winter,
1953), 13.

really are, but as they seem or as they might be : "nothing more than a Representation, or, as *Aristotle* calls it, an Imitation of what really exists" (*Tom Jones*, VII, i).

On one occasion he startles the modern reader by seeming to anticipate Coleridge's insistence on the deliberate effort required to transcend the unrealities of art, "that willing suspension of disbelief . . . which constitutes poetic faith." In *Tom Jones* Fielding writes of a vital "Poetic Faith" which allows sophisticated readers to suspend disbelief in what "hath not occurred to their own Observation." His discussion of "Poetic Faith," which continues through eighteen paragraphs, is amusingly presented, with some purposely absurd illustrations. When in the same discussion he quotes "a Genius of the highest Rank" as saying that "The great art of all Poetry is to mix Truth with Fiction; in order to join the Credible with the Surprizing," the "Genius" turns out to be that imaginary polymath Martinus Scriblerus in his *Treatise on the Art of Sinking in Poetry* (*Tom Jones*, VIII, i). Unlike Aristotle, Coleridge, and modern "serious" critics of literature, Fielding liked to make significant critical observations in the guise of horseplay, and to make intentionally fallacious critical jokes look like significant pronouncements — another way of "playing the reader like a trout" and testing his powers of discrimination.[4]

In the essays which follow this Introduction I have not attempted to trace or even to identify the influences that led Fielding to dwell on the nature of reality and to employ wit and humor in an attack on folly and vice. W. B. Coley, again, writes that "The example of South, the aesthetic of Shaftesbury and the practice of Swift confirm the availability for Fielding of a tradition of 'wit.'"[5] As Coley points out, it was a tradition involv-

---

[4] See Ernest Dilworth, "Fielding and Coleridge," *Notes and Queries,* CCIII (January, 1958), 35–37.

[5] W. B. Coley, "The Background of Fielding's Laughter," *ELH,* XXVI (June, 1959), 252.

ing what Swift termed "the sin of wit" : an audacious preference for ridicule, parody, and laughter in the attempt to effect moral ends, eschewing long-faced gravity and pulpit rhetoric. In his essay, "Satiric and Comic Theory in Relation to Fielding," A. E. Dyson assesses Fielding's use of Shaftesbury's doctrine, that ridicule is a "test of truth"; and he remarks that although "in his earlier writings Fielding's aims were satiric and his techniques greatly influenced by Swift," the Swiftian influence gives way, in the later fiction, to the less severe comic mode.[6]

Nor have I made a separate study of the exact doctrinal nature of Fielding's moral purpose, although "moral purpose" is everywhere in the fiction, whether explicitly announced or not. This subject has been notably treated in J. A. Work's essay, "Henry Fielding, Christian Censor," George Sherburn's essay, "Fielding's Social Outlook," and M. C. Battestin's *The Moral Basis of Fielding's Art: A Study of "Joseph Andrews."* All three show the fundamental morality, exaltation of "good nature," and latitudinarian benevolism in the fiction. J. Middleton Murry defended the responsible morality of the "great" works, *Tom Jones* and *Amelia.* And, it seems to me surprising, William Empson, to whom one turns for illumination on ambiguities and verbal structures, preferred to devote most of his study of *Tom Jones* to a defense of Tom's morals.[7]

I want to suggest how, in his fiction, Henry Fielding attempted vigorously and cheerfully to define the good life, within the severe limitations set by Fortune, society, and man's own errant

---

[6] A. E. Dyson, *Modern Language Quarterly,* XVIII (September, 1957), 225 ff.

[7] J. A. Work, "Henry Fielding, Christian Censor," *The Age of Johnson: Essays Presented to C. B. Tinker* (New Haven, 1949), pp. 139–148; George Sherburn, "Fielding's Social Outlook," *Philological Quarterly,* XXXV (January, 1956), 1–23; M. C. Battestin, *The Moral Basis of Fielding's Art: A Study of "Joseph Andrews"* (Middletown, Conn., 1959); J. Middleton Murry, "In Defence of Fielding," *Unprofessional Essays* (London, 1956), pp. 11–52; William Empson, "Tom Jones," *Kenyon Review,* XX (Spring, 1958), 217–249.

nature. As a religious man, man of law, and author, Fielding respected the power of the word. Human and literary themes frequently run parallel in his fiction, sometimes crossing or converging. The state of the arts, especially those arts involving the written word, was for Fielding a clue to the condition of society — a clue to man's real idea of himself in relation to the universe and other human beings. He agreed with Pope in *The Dunciad* that the eternal darkness (which threatens to cover all things) shows itself first in the debasement and denigration of the "creating Word."

Putting emphasis on his concern with life, literature, and the feigning through which life and literature seem to merge their identities, I try to interpret part of Fielding's achievement for the modern reader. By means of explication I look into some of the amusing devices and serious underlying intentions of his prose fiction; and I insist upon an appreciation of the fiction as art.

After working through *Shamela*'s literary relationships, which are preposterously funny but tryingly complicated, we emerge into the bright "real" world of Fielding's three major works.

I

The Art of Parody

Shamela

The Pamela, which he abused in his Shamela, taught him how to write to please, tho' his manners are so different.—Samuel Richardson.[1]

Few parodies can withstand more than one rereading. But the energetic fun that went into the composition of *An Apology for the Life of Mrs. Shamela Andrews* (1741) keeps it fresh even after it has become familiar. Fun, though it may be abusive or finally at the expense of the reader himself, is the distinguishing characteristic of successful parody. Laughter, the reader's first reaction, issues from recognition and is succeeded by appreciation for the parodist's aptness, wit, and daring. In the few great parodies this entertainment is not diminished by a general criticism of literature and life—upon which the greatness, as distinguished from mere "hitting it off," largely depends. One of the important parodies of prose fiction in English, *Shamela* amusingly and tellingly distorts its models in minute details; but the reader does not have to be aware of those details, or even to have read Richardson's *Pamela,* its foremost model, to share much of the sport and to recognize most of the oblique truths in *Shamela.*

Triumph of parody is never more laughingly evident, or more

---

[1] Samuel Richardson to " Mrs. Belfour," Lady Bradshaigh, 1749, *Correspondence,* ed. Anna Barbauld (London, 1804), IV, 286.

critically efficacious, than when it contrives on a single page not only to isolate and magnify the absurdities of a work at hand, and to demonstrate weaknesses of the literary kind represented by that work, but also contrives to show the incongruities between fictional characters as they are drawn by literary convention and as they would appear in terms of life, perhaps going further to hint at discrepancies between the codes and conventions by which we pretend to live and the antics we perform as human animals.

In *The Tragedy of Tragedies; or, The Life and Death of Tom Thumb the Great* (1730, altered in 1731), Fielding had parodied the absurdities of heroic and quasi-heroic plays. It remains the best line-for-line take-off in English drama, "replete," as Fielding's first biographer said of it, " with as fine parody as perhaps, has ever been written."[2] But *Tom Thumb*, meticulously specific though it is in quarrying from more than forty tragedies identified by Fielding in burlesque footnotes, maintains its strength of fascination because it has a good deal to say about all pretentiousness and inanity, not necessarily dramatic. The parodied Preface and footnotes invite one to see how the pretentious and inane look under the heading of literary scholarship. They look, of course, familiar. If the "tragic" text of *Tom Thumb* seems familiar, with its theme of Love-and-Honour, its blazing hero, its inflammable heroine, its violence and bombast, these conventionally familiar elements are at once jerked into grotesque distortion; for the hero is a manikin, the heroine bears the preposterous name of Huncamunca, the hero is eaten (offstage) by a red cow, and at the end everyone kills everyone else, leaving the King to commit suicide: "Ha! murderess vile, take that. (*Kills* Mustacha.) And take thou this. (*Kills himself and falls.*)" Rhetoric murders rhetoric itself.

Part of the fun of reading *Tom Thumb* is in observing the act of parody in process: through quotations cited in his footnotes

---

[2] Arthur Murphy, " Essay on the Life and Genius of Henry Fielding, Esq," *Works of Fielding,* 2nd ed. (London, 1762), I, 26.

it is easy to trace Fielding's method. Sometimes phrases are drawn intact into the text; ambiguous phrasing is pushed in the direction of the absurd or indecent; proportions and emphases are wickedly altered, perhaps by addition of a single contaminating word; exalted flights of rhetoric are juxtaposed with "low" phrasing. Thus, Nathaniel Lee's pretentious conceit "Dost thou not view joy peeping from my eyes,/ The casements open'd wide to gaze on thee?" is altered to "your eyes,/ That like the open windows us'd to shew/ The lovely beauty of the rooms within,/ Have now two blinds before them." Lee's casements are logically extended to provide a view, and then particularized by window-coverings, only surrealistically now retaining the aptness of the "eye" metaphor. The sound is almost authentic; the sense, with only the slightest tampering, has turned mad.

Similarly, parody-in-process is observable in some of Fielding's essays in the *Champion* which criticize infelicities in the Poet Laureate's autobiography, just published. In the *Champion* for Tuesday, 29 April 1740, Fielding ironically identifies the Laureate as "one of the *Greatest Writers* of our own Age : I mean Mr. *Colley Cibber,* who, in the Apology for his Life, tells us, that *we have frequently Great Writers that cannot read.*" Pretending to illustrate how Cibber himself can neither read nor write, Fielding quotes verbatim examples of awkward grammar and vocabulary, following these with some of Cibber's attempts at sublimity of style, displayed as though in a gallery of bad art. Three months later many of these objectionable quotations reappeared, this time in the book-length parody called *An Apology for the Life of Mr. T*[heophilus] *C*[ibber], in which Fielding's influence or hand shows up. The method of this leg-pull, purporting to be the work of the Laureate's son, is chiefly that of direct quotation, often unaltered, to suggest that Cibber had unwittingly devised his own parody. Cibber's language is adopted or mimicked until the parodist is ready, with some little alteration, to render it not only laughable but lunatic, appropriate to the man who was to

become immortal in the role of the hero of *The Dunciad*. Cibber
had written that " Beauty, like the Sun, must sometimes lose its
Power to chuse, and shine into equal Warmth, the Peasant and
the Courtier" (*Apology*, p. 42). Fielding, in the *Champion*,
objects that " When in page 42. we read, Beauty SHINES INTO
equal Warmth the Peasant and the Courtier, do we not know
what he means though he hath made a Verb active of SHINE."
In the parody it becomes " *Beauty, like the Sun, shines into equal
Warmth, the Peasant and the Courtier* " (p. 29). Through
omission of the phrase between the words "Sun" and "shine" as
Cibber had it, confusion is intentionally added to strain further
the conceit and wayward grammar. Again, Cibber had written
that " Mrs. *Oldfield* having thrown out such new Proffers of a
Genius, I was no longer at a loss for Support" (p. 176). Objecting
to "Proffers" as a noun, Fielding cites this in the *Champion*
merely as "*Mrs*. Oldfield *threw out such new Proffers of a
Genius*." But the reference becomes arrogantly personal as well
as ungrammatical in the parody : "nor did I fling out the Proffer
of any great *Genius*" (p. 65).

Like the heroic dramas burlesqued in *Tom Thumb*, Colley
Cibber's *Apology* at its worst, in its most unleashed rhetoric,
anticipates the parodist's art; and to some extent this is true of
Samuel Richardson's epistolary *Pamela* : *or, Virtue Rewarded*
(November, 1740). When the servant girl Pamela, by patiently
twisting or fainting away from her employer's amorous advances,
has been breath-takingly elevated to the state of marriage, she
writes how, " the Ceremony of the Ring passing next, I receiv'd
the dear Favour, at his worthy Hands, with a most grateful
Heart; and he was pleased to say afterwards in the Chariot, That
when he had done saying, *With this Ring I thee wed,* &c. I
made a Court'sy, and said, Thank you, Sir. May-be I did; for I
am sure it was a most grateful Part of the Service" (II, p. 144).[3]

---

[3] Identifications of passages from *Pamela* are made by reference to the
numbered letters (Letter xii, etc.) through Letter xxxi; after that point, because

Even the most entranced readers of Pamela's letters, even the
clergymen who preached sermons on their moral charms, must
have felt the burlesque of that passage, which would be hard to
improve upon as an example of self-conscious, simpering humility
at the moment of achieving a calculated social, monetary, and
sexual triumph.

But surely much of the genuine astonishment that accompanies
a sympathetic reading of *Pamela* today derives from Richardson's
adroit anticipation of almost every objection that might be made,
thematic, technical, or psychological. The practical impossibility
of such voracious letter- and journal-writing, much of it "to the
Moment," is almost immediately remarked upon by Mr. B., the
vexedly prurient employer, who is intrigued and a little alarmed
at such indefatigable penmanship; and when Pamela herself
writes that " it will be said, I blab every thing " (Letter xvi), she
has exactly framed the opinion, not only of Mr. B., but of the
reader and—to give him credit—Samuel Richardson. Because
Pamela's idea of virtue seems limited, almost exclusively in important matters, to the immuring of chastity against violation
before marriage, there is naturally much concern with sex in her
letters. With Mr. B. on her mind, she dreams that she is pursued
by a bull, and even the milk-cow seems a bull to her, exciting her
to a state of terror. Her account of poor, frustrated Mr. B.'s
attempt at rape is oddly ambiguous : "I found his Hand in my
Bosom, and when my Fright let me know it, I was ready to die;
and I sighed, and screamed, and fainted away. And still he had
his Arms about my Neck" (Letter xxv). Though ostensibly

Richardson alters the strictly epistolary form to that of a running journal,
references must be made to volume and page. Fielding parodies the 2nd ed.,
which differs widely from the 1st. All quotations from *Pamela* here are from
the Shakespeare Head Ed. (Oxford, 1929), based on the 6th ed., but not
significantly different—in the quoted passages—from the 2nd ed. used by
Fielding. For the novel's prefatory matter in the 2nd ed., however, I have
used the facsimile reproduction in *Samuel Richardson's Introduction to
"Pamela,"* ed. Sheridan W. Baker, Jr., Augustan Reprint Soc. Publ. No. 48
(Los Angeles, 1954).

intended for the edification of her old parents, her detailed
description is a source of pleasure to herself, Richardson, and the
reader; but how, one's curiosity is tickled to know, was she aware
of Mr. B.'s arms when she had fainted? Such ambiguities lead
Mr. B., after only a few pages, to announce that, while he finds
her lovely, "I take her to be an artful young Baggage" (Letter
xiv); and later, "See, said he, and took the Glass with one Hand,
and turn'd me round with the other, What a Shape! what a
Neck! what a Hand! and what a Bloom in that lovely Face! —
But who can describe the Tricks and Artifices, that lie lurking in
her little, plotting, guileful Heart! 'Tis no Wonder the poor
Parson was infatuated with her!" (I, pp. 252–253). In the latter
speech Richardson shrewdly anticipates, through Mr. B., any
reader's suspicion that Pamela Andrews is too good to be true.
In that speech, supposedly scribbled down in haste by Pamela
herself, Richardson allows her to tot up her own physical attractions at the risk of sounding vain in excess; and he allows the
reader to speculate, by means of the strong word "infatuated,"
on the true nature of Parson Williams, who proposed marriage to
Pamela and of whom Mr. B. is somewhat jealous. It is this little
parson whom Fielding ruthlessly alters into Pamela's paramour,
father of her child out of wedlock, and cuckolder of Mr. B[ooby].

For although Fielding's method of parody in the *Apology for
the Life of Mrs. Shamela Andrews* is to make fun of *Pamela* by
debasement, it generally operates by leaping upon incongruities
of characterization and plot already pointed out, in one way or
another throughout the letters, by Richardson himself. Because
the main business of the two full volumes of *Pamela* is represented in fewer than fifty pages in *Shamela,* the shock to the
reader is set off, not only by funny, distorted exaggeration, but by
sheer concentration of Richardson's story. In Shamela's initial
letter, for instance, Fielding hastens the action and pulls together
material that extended as far as Letter xxxi in *Pamela.*

LETTER I

SHAMELA ANDREWS *to Mrs.* HENRIETTA MARIA HON-
ORA ANDREWS *at her Lodgings at the* Fan *and* Pepper-Box *in*
Drury-Lane.

Dear Mamma,

This comes to acquaint you, that I shall set out in the Waggon
on *Monday,* desiring you to commodate me with a Ludgin, as near
you as possible, in *Coulstin's-Court,* or *Wild-Street,* or somewhere
thereabouts; pray let it be handsome, and not above two Stories
high : For Parson *Williams* hath promised to visit me when he
comes to Town, and I have got a good many fine Cloaths of the
Old Put my Mistress's, who died a wil ago; and I beleve Mrs.
Jervis will come along with me, for she says she would like to keep
a House somewhere about *Short's-Gardens,* or towards *Queen-*
Street; and if there was convenience for a *Bannio,* she should like
it the better; but that she will settle herself when she comes to
Town.—*O ! How I long to be in the Balconey at the Old House—*
so no more at present from

Your affectionate Daughter,
SHAMELA.

Unlike Richardson's heroine, who wrote accurately and sometimes with professional slickness, this girl misspells as any lady's
maid in her nonage would be expected to; but otherwise her
letters show her to be an unexpected, vulgar horror—though a
most amusing horror. Richardson's model heroine began her
initial letter in similar fashion ("I have great Trouble, and some
Comfort, to acquaint you with"); but it was not until her thirty-
first letter that she got around to the source for the rest of
Shamela's first sentence ("I will set out To-morrow early; and the
Honour you design'd me, as Mrs. *Jervis* tells me, of your Chariot,
there will be no Occasion for; because I can hire, I believe, Farmer *Brady's* Chaise"). The same letter in *Pamela* mentioned the

name of the parson ("if it were but to ask his Advice about Mr.
Williams"). Then to find the source for Shamela's reference to
her dead mistress' "fine Cloaths," one must turn back to Letter
vi in *Pamela,* where there is an account of "my late Lady's
Cloaths," of " fine Silk, and too rich and too good for me, to be
sure." Mrs. Jervis's hankering, in Fielding's parody, to "keep a
House" or bagnio stems from the perfectly respectable wish of
the original Mrs. Jervis, in Letter xii of *Pamela,* " to live inde-
pendent; then she would take a little private House, and I should
live with her like her Daughter." And in Letter xii, too, when
Pamela exclaimed, " O that I had never left my little Bed in the
Loft . . !" she set the pattern, though not the (im)moral tone for
Shamela's *"O! How I long to be in the Balconey at the Old
House."*

That is the first of Shamela's epistolary exclamations, most of
them coarse, bored, and impatient, such as "O! What precious
Fools Men are!" and *"O what a silly Fellow is a bashful young
Lover!"* Similarly exclamatory were Pamela's outcries in her
letters, characterized however by self-pitying but patient piety,
like " O why are poor foolish Maidens try'd with such Dangers,
when they have such weak Minds to grapple with them!" and
(rather wordily censorious) "O the unparallel'd Wickedness,
Stratagems, and Devices of those who call themselves Gentlemen,
yet pervert the Design of Providence, in giving them ample
Means to do Good, to their everlasting Perdition, and the Ruin
of poor oppressed Innocence!" By inversion of these sentiments,
Fielding provokes in the reader an amused impatience with
Pamela's "O the unparallel'd Wickedness," which seems to contribute as little to an intelligent conduct of life as do the brash
opinions of Shamela.

LETTERS II–V

Letter ii in *Shamela* returns to Richardson's first letter for its
account of how the young employer " took me by the Hand, and

I pretended to be shy" (in *Pamela* he "took my by the Hand; yes, he took my Hand before them all"); but for the kisses that immediately follow, Fielding has drawn on a later episode. Shamela's vexation at interruption of the love-play is, of course, Fielding's own contribution. And the brief Letters iii and v, from Shamela's mother, as well as Shamela's equally brief Letter iv, are mostly Fielding's invention to move his story along, though there are possibly some unimportant echoed phrases, such as "I read in good Books" (Letter iv), reminiscent of "all she loves to hear read is good Books" in Letter v of *Pamela*.

LETTER VI

Letter vi, set down in three installments in *Shamela*, clearly shows Fielding's critical method of selection and alteration. One source of psychological convincingness in *Pamela* was Richardson's occasional curdling of poor Mr. B.'s ill-received amatory overtures into tantrums of name-calling directed at the object of his love. Here Shamela reports to her mother how Mr. Booby

caught me in his Arms, and kissed me till he made my Face all over Fire. Now this served purely you know, to put upon the Fool for Anger. O! What precious Fools Men are! And so I flung from him in a mighty Rage, and pretended as how I would go out at the Door ; but when I came to the End of the Room, I stood still, and my Master cryed out, Hussy, Slut, Saucebox, Boldface, come hither . . . .

In her Letter xi Richardson's Pamela had told how Mr. B. kissed her "two or three times, with frightful Eagerness" and exasperatedly called her a "foolish Hussy" and a "foolish Slut." Later, in Letter xv, Pamela was called "Saucebox" and "Bold-face"; and Mr. B. "offer'd to take me on his Knee, with some Force," "by Force kissed my Neck and Lips," and "then put his Hand into my Bosom," after which, according to Pamela, her indignation gave her strength to wrench "free from him by a

sudden Spring" and she ran from the room. The key to the parody
here resides in Fielding's words "pretended as how"; for although
Shamela makes a calculated show of indignation and does not
want to leave the room, Pamela did run from it in spite of her
desire for Mr. B.— in marriage. This passage in *Shamela*
continues with the girl's impertinent reply to Mr. Booby:

Yes to be sure, says I; why don't you come, says he; what should
I come for says I; if you don't come to me, I'll come to you, says
he; I shan't come to you I assure you, says I. Upon which he run
up, caught me in his Arms, and flung me upon a Chair, and began
to offer to touch my Under-Petticoat. Sir, says I, you had better
not offer to be rude; well, says he, no more I won't then; and away
he went out of the Room. I was so mad to be sure I could have
cry'd. . . . Mrs. *Jervis* who had been without, harkening, now came
to me. She burst into a violent Laugh the Moment she came in.

 " Began to offer to touch my Under-Petticoat," altered from
"offer'd to take me on his Knee," represents in detail Shamela's
satisfaction, up to that point, with Mr. Booby's progress in wooing.
But her pretense of outraged innocence, taken seriously by Mr.
Booby, results in disappointment for her. The original Mrs. Jervis,
far from being moved to laughter by this episode, " could not
speak for crying" (Letter xv).

Shamela's second installment of Letter vi, in imitation of some
of Pamela's journal-letters, is headed *"Thursday Night, Twelve
o'Clock"* and opens with a deserved burlesque of the epistolary
style which fuses action with the written report of that action. In
this matter, too, Richardson anticipated parody, for it would be
hard to write any more directly "to the Moment" than in
Pamela's accounts of hearing footsteps behind her as she moves
her pen across the paper to describe them. Shamela, somehow
managing pen and paper, rapidly writes:

Mrs. *Jervis* and I are just in Bed, and the Door unlocked; if my
Master should come—Odsbobs! I hear him just coming at the
Door. You see I write in the present Tense, as Parson *Williams* says.

Well, he is in Bed between us, we both shamming a Sleep, he steals his Hand into my Bosom, which I, as if in my Sleep, press close to me with mine, and then pretend to awake.

Recognizing her cue, after having planned the entire scene with Mrs. Jervis, Shamela screams, scratches, and counterfeits a swoon. Mrs. Jervis cries out that the girl has been murdered. Frightened, Mr. Booby abandons his attack and, when Shamela finally pretends to recover her senses, begs her forgiveness, saying that "by Heaven, I know not whether you are a Man or a Woman, unless by your swelling Breasts." But before he leaves, he has again been reduced to name-calling. Most of this, except the open pretense — Shamela's shamming — derives from Letter xxv in *Pamela,* where Mr. B., driven desperate, made an attack on the girl in the bed she shared with Mrs. Jervis. But it was in this scene that Pamela, who supposedly scorned pretense, after telling how she "found his Hand in my Bosom" and then "screamed, and fainted away," went on to say that "still he had his Arms about my Neck." Fielding has had only to confirm the pretense, and depict sham as a policy and way of life, to reduce Richardson's episode from virtuousness to vulgarity. In the original, when Mrs. Jervis shrieked that "my poor *Pamela* is dead for certain!" her utterance came from anxiety, not from rehearsals. For Mr. Booby's vow that he had not ventured beyond Shamela's "swelling Breasts," Fielding reaches ahead in *Pamela* to another episode where Mr. B. vowed that "I know not, I declare (beyond this lovely Bosom), your Sex" (I, p. 282).

Headed "*Friday Morning,*" the third section of Letter vi tells how Mrs. Jervis and Shamela are instructed to quit Mr. Booby's employ: the "morning after" has brought him to a state of impatience with both female servants. But Shamela, her head full of plans, insists to Mrs. Jervis that "I'll warrant we are not so near being turned away, as you imagine." In Richardson's *Pamela,* on the night of the attack, Mr. B. had threatened Mrs. Jervis with violence and wanted "to turn her out of the House the next Morning" (Letter xxv); the next day, when Mrs. Jervis begged to take Pamela with her, Mr. B. told her "the sooner the better." Referring to Mrs. Jervis's plight, Pamela simply expressed a "hope it may still be made up" (Letter xxvi).

Thus, action in Letter vi of Fielding's semi-obscene parody faithfully, and in detail, parallels an episode in Richardson's novel (which announced on its title page a lofty intention "to cultivate the Principles of VIRTUE and RELIGION in the Minds of the YOUTH of BOTH SEXES"). The vital difference between the novel and the parody here is that Fielding has caused his heroine to state her conniving intentions openly and proudly, letting her crudely announce that she "pretended as how," is "shamming," and plans "a Fetch" for Mr. Booby, with no idea of leaving his house without wifely access to his moneybags.

Although Richardson daringly allowed Mr. B. to accuse his heroine of all the shamming that Fielding's heroine embodies and admits to, he preserved to the end Pamela's reputation for undeviating Christian goodness, which she herself more than once remarked upon. The possibility that Pamela was vain, affected, hypocritical, and calculating—truly the "subtle, artful Gipsey" that Mr. B. once called her—hovers persistently but elusively over the pages, suspended there almost invisibly by means of Richardson's considerable art. Pamela seemed to remain decently passive in her "hope" that Mr. B. would not evict Mrs. Jervis; Shamela, indecently active, by plotting with Mrs. Jervis against Mr. Booby, makes their eviction unlikely. And the episode concludes, in both novel and parody, with the heroine signing her epistle as a "Dutiful Daughter." Duty, in the novel, is to please impoverished old parents by maintaining Virtue until it can be Rewarded; in the parody, Duty is to please a mother, who formerly "sold Oranges in the Play-House," by securing the Reward by whatever means, even by shamming Virtue.

LETTERS VII–XI

Two episodes from *Pamela* are altered and joined in Fielding's Letter vii, "*Mrs.* LUCRETIA JERVIS *to* HENRIETTA MARIA HONORA ANDREWS." The account of how Shamela, in neat rural dress, bamboozles Mr. Booby closely imitates Richardson's Letter xxiv. And the account of Mr. Booby's plan to abduct Shamela to his Lincolnshire estate is drawn from interpolated remarks by Richardson in his role as "Editor," following Letter xxxi in *Pamela*. In *Shamela,* the disguise as a farmer's daughter is represented as the conniving "Fetch" (now called her "Stratagem") alluded to in Letter vi; and the abduction to Lincolnshire is no surprise to her, for Shamela has been informed, and is delighted to return to the scene where she had her child by Parson Williams and where she will renew acquaintance with "our old Friend *Nanny Jewkes*," a benign version of the grotesque Mrs. Jewkes who kept Pamela a prisoner.

Just as Pamela industriously copied out letters and documents to swell the bulk of her history, intended for her parents to read, Shamela encloses a letter from Parson Williams in her Letter ix and a transcript of a letter from him, itself transcribing his letter to Mr. Booby, in her Number xii. In her Number x she transcribes a letter from Mr. Booby, who announces that "I cannot live without you," an echo of Mr. B.'s plea when he represented himself as "one that cannot live without you, and on whose Honour to you, you may absolutely depend " (I, p. 178).

Shamela's reaction to this avowal is to enumerate the advantages of being Mrs. Booby — the estate, coaches, house in London, servants, the jewels that are almost within her grasp. She jeopardizes her future, however, by a rendezvous in the garden with Parson Williams, and to provide an excuse for her absence from the house,

it came into my Head to pretend as how I intended to drown myself; so I stript off one of my Petticoats, and threw it into the

Canal; and then I went and hid myself in the Coal-hole, where I lay all Night; and comforted myself with repeating over some Psalms, and other good things, which I had got by heart. (Letter x)

When Shamela's petticoat is found in the water, the servants bring out a drag-net; but she is discovered amongst the coal and is led into the house for breakfast. This is a variation on a scene in which Richardson's Pamela, stripping off her upper petticoat, neck handkerchief, and cap, flung them into the pond in order to be thought drowned and to divert her pursuers when, with the key in her possession, she planned to unlock the wall door and escape; but discovering that the lock had been changed, Pamela hid, "low and dejected," in the woodhouse. Before she was discovered there, where the frantic thought of suicide occurred to her, a drag-net was ordered for her search (I, pp. 227–240).

This pretended drowning of the heroine, with motives quite opposed in the novel and in the parody, is followed by still another effort to rape her. In both versions, with Mrs. Jewkes holding one of the heroine's arms, and Mr. B[ooby] "as rude as possible," there is a struggle on the bed. "What you do, Sir, do; don't stand dilly-dallying," cried Richardson's Mrs. Jewkes. "Why don't you do it? I have one Arm secure, if you can't deal with the rest I am sorry for you," cries Fielding's Mrs. Jewkes. (In this instance it seems to me that the model is funnier than the parody.) But whereas Pamela conveniently fainted away, Shamela discourages poor Mr. Booby by following her mother's instructions, forcefully grasping his privates with her free hand : *" O Parson Williams, how little are all the Men in the World compared to thee."* In both versions, too, there is a proposal from Mr. B[ooby] to settle money and other advantages on the heroine if she becomes his mistress; for both the heroines, Shamela replies a little vulgarly by saying that " I value my Vartue more than all the World, and I had rather be the poorest Man's Wife than the richest Man's Whore." She pushes further, however, to state explicitly what a Pamela could never trust to paper : " I thought once of making a little Fortune by my Person. I now intend to make a great one by my Vartue."

The remaining eighteen pages of Shamela's correspondence, though written at different times, are under the heading of "Letter xii," just as the last four-fifths of *Pamela,* after Letter xxxi, assumed the form of a journal. During a walk in the garden Mr. Booby takes Shamela's hand, remarks on his jealousy of Parson Williams, and asks her to "suppose I should lay aside all Considerations of Fortune, and disregard the Censure of the World, and marry you." Surprisingly, Shamela demurs. In the original of this scene, Mr. B. took Pamela's hand in the garden, expressed a jealousy which made him "hate the Name of *Williams,*" and achieved anti-climax by protesting, still unwilling to bestow the Reward upon lowly Virtue, "But my dear Girl, what must we do about the World, and the World's Censure? — Indeed, I cannot marry!" (I, p. 300).

One more scene precedes Shamela's marriage. Preparing to return to her mother, though suspecting that Mr. Booby will send after her (as he finally does), and prepared to "brazen it out," as she says, Shamela flings herself into the chariot, and is driven off. Pamela had also ridden away from Mr. B. in a chariot. Before either girl travels very far, a man on horseback comes at "full Speed" with a letter, Shamela's being from Parson Williams, who has been arrested (like the original Williams), and Pamela's being a conciliatory plea from Mr. B.

On the wedding night, Shamela simulates bashful virginity, even shamming a blush "by holding my Breath, and squeezing my Cheeks," to achieve something like Pamela's description of how she trembled and her "Colour went and came." Both husbands, though eager, allot their brides time alone in their closets before going to bed, Shamela utilizing her quarter of an hour to

write to Parson Williams, and Pamela writing out her more
generous half hour in a letter to her parents. Their marriages
now consummated, both brides are rewarded by the pay-off. On
the next day Pamela received fifty guineas for her parents' debts
and a hundred more for the servants; when she begged to give a
guinea to "a poor Body in the Town," Mr. B. magnanimously
replied, "Send Two, my Dear, if you please" (II, p. 172).
Shamela immediately distributes her hundred guineas among the
servants and asks for another hundred, fifty of which she sends
to Parson Williams; on the next day she wants a third hundred
guineas but, to get it, has to throw a fit.

"I forgot to mention, that Mr. *Williams* was here Yesterday,"
Pamela remarked, perhaps too casually, in the midst of her
epistolary report on her first bridal days. After the wedding
Parson Williams, who had served as a kind of half-hearted foil
for Mr. B., withdrew almost entirely from the story. In Shamela's
story, however, Parson Williams now dominates over Mr. Booby,
sharing the adulterous spoils with his loved one. To dramatize
Williams's unpriestly proclivities, Fielding takes hints from an
episode that occurred in *Pamela* before the marriage, when
Pamela and Mr. B., out for a drive, encountered Parson Williams
walking in the meadow and invited him into the coach with them.
At the request of Mr. B., who was evidently trying to prove that
he had conquered jealousy, Parson Williams kissed Pamela's
hand, sat next to her ("all that ever he could do," Richardson
has her say!), and rode with them to dine "in a most pleasant,
and easy, and frank manner" (II, pp. 87–94). Quite differently,
the parson when encountered in *Shamela* is not walking in the
meadow but is poaching Mr. Booby's hares; the two men exchange places, actually and symbolically, Booby following on
horseback while the parson rides in the coach, kisses the bride,
inquires about the wedding night, and discourses on the difference
between Flesh and Spirit; at dinner he accepts Mr. Booby's note

for fifty pounds and promises to pray for him. This is something like the business of Restoration comedy. And indeed Fielding's *Grub-Street Opera* (1731), in the Restoration mode, had featured both a Parson Puzzletext, "in love with women, tobacco, drink, and backgammon," and a young gentleman in pursuit of a serving maid, with a good deal of talk, ironically intended, about the "value of virtue" : the butler in the play entreated Sweetissa, "if you love virtue—if you love honour—if you have humanity, answer me one question. Did the parson ever make love to you?" (III, vii).

In the opinion of Charles B. Woods, the reprimanding of the clergy is one of the major themes in *Shamela*. The moral duty of the clergy, Fielding's topic for several essays in the *Champion* in the year preceding *Shamela*, now appears as a subject to be remarked upon satirically and incorporated with the burlesque of Richardson's "moral" novel. Williams's danger to the church and to society is represented not only by his lechery but by his doctrinal division of Flesh and Spirit, exaggerated here to justify Shamela's retaining a paramour to satisfy her desire while her husband provides "those other Conveniences." Mr. Woods shows that Parson Williams is intended to portray "the kind of clergyman who agreed with Whitefield and Wesley on the question of Faith vs. Good Works."[4] This comment has been glossed by Ian Watt, who says that " Fielding's religious target in *Shamela*, however, is certainly not the Methodists as such, but rather those of any persuasion who are governed by what in *Joseph Andrews* he called 'the detestable doctrine of faith against good works.'"[5] Both Mr. Woods and Mr. Watt dwell at length on the significance and sources for Williams's sermon text "*Be not Righteous over-much.*" But like almost everything else in the body of *Shamela*,

---

[4] Charles B. Woods, "Fielding and the Authorship of *Shamela,*" *Philological Quarterly*, XXV (July, 1946), 264.
[5] Ian Watt, Introduction, *An Apology for the Life of Mrs. Shamela Andrews,* Augustan Reprint Soc. Publ. No. 57 (Los Angeles, 1956), p. 7.

that text comes directly from *Pamela*, 2nd ed. (the fifth prefatory letter).[6]

Concurring with Poetic Justice, the authority of Ecclesiastical Law has the last word in *Shamela*; for Fielding arrives at a Finis more sternly moral than Richardson's, not by rewarding Virtue, but by punishing Hypocrisy :

I have a certain Account, that Mr. *Booby* hath caught his Wife in bed with *Williams*; hath turned her off, and is prosecuting him in the spiritual Court.

For the sake of convenience, and after experimenting with other, clumsier approaches, I have handled the stories of Pamela and Shamela here as though their relationship is that of an original work and its imitation in the form of parody. But one of Fielding's funniest devices is his assurance to the reader that *Shamela* is the truth and that *Pamela* was concocted for money by a professional writer of Histories, who invented flattering lives "out of his own Head" and "*can make black white*, it seems." To insist upon the variegated coloring of human nature, the parodist opposes one kind of extreme with another. The "true" Pamela is Shamela, we are entertainingly told in Shamela's final postscript and in the introduction and conclusion to her narrative, in the form of letters between two parsons.

LETTERS OF TICKLETEXT AND OLIVER

These three letters, of Parson Tickletext and Parson Oliver, together with a letter of "The EDITOR to *Himself*" and a letter from "JOHN PUFF, *Esq*; *to the* EDITOR," mimic the thirty-six pages of matter introductory to the second edition of *Pamela* : Richardson's Preface, followed by adulatory or critical readers' letters, some of them represented by abstracts or excerpts.

The first letter of Parson Tickletext to Parson Oliver recom-

[6] This is noted by Sheridan W. Baker, Jr., Introduction, *An Apology for the Life of Mrs. Shamela Andrews* (Berkeley and Los Angeles, 1953), p. xv.

mends *Pamela* as an immortal work, a model for daughters and servant-maids, and a text for the pulpit. Into this letter Fielding has woven numerous lines of direct quotation from Richardson's introductory matter : this was the technique in *An Apology for the Life of Mr. T*[heophilus] *C*[ibber]; and it is of course like Richardson's own printing of excerpts from letters prefatory to *Pamela*. But some of these quotations, though they begin verbatim like Richardson's, amusingly go wrong in the direction of vulgarity. Whereas one of Richardson's admirers had exclaimed, " Little Book, charming PAMELA! face the World, and never doubt of finding Friends and Admirers, not only in thine own Country, but far from Home," Fielding rudely alters it to " Little Book, charming *Pamela*, get thee gone; face the World, in which thou wilt find nothing like thyself." Or, by the device of omission, "this *Father, of Millions of* MINDS" preposterously reads "this Father of Millions." Or whereas Richardson's imagination was described as having prodigiously "stretched out this diminutive mere *Grain of Mustard-seed,* (a poor Girl's little, innocent, Story) into a Resemblance of That *Heaven,* which the Best of Good Books has compar'd it to," in *Shamela* there is the wicked, catastrophic substitution of "a poor Girl's little, *&c.*"

Parson Oliver's reply to Parson Tickletext expresses his disappointment that such extravagant, unthinking praise should be laid before so patent a hoax as *Pamela*. Heaven help the clergy, he says, if " the Cause of Religion, or Morality, can want such slender Support." Anyway, he adds, the heroine's real name is not Pamela but Shamela, and he is forwarding to Parson Tickletext the papers which compose the authentic narrative. Phrases from various portions of Richardson's introductory matter turn up in Parson Oliver's delusion-shattering paragraphs, and he proves that *Pamela* does not represent its author's starry-eyed innocence :

I cannot agree that my Daughter should entertain herself with some of his Pictures; which I do not expect to be contemplated without Emotion, unless by one of my Age and Temper, who can see the Girl lie on her Back, with one Arm round Mrs. *Jewkes* and the other round the Squire, naked in Bed, with his Hand on her Breasts, *&c.* with as much Indifference as I read any other Page in the whole Novel.

This faithful summary of one scene from *Pamela* serves a purpose, through contrast, of drawing attention to the strongest objection that Richardson allowed to appear in his introductory matter, the insipid complaint that " the Passage where the Gentleman is said to span the Waist of Pamela with his Hand " may encourage tight-lacing among females!

When he has transcribed all the letters comprising the story, Parson Oliver says, " So much for Mrs. *Shamela, or Pamela,*" but goes on to argue for the letters' publication as a useful warning to young gentlemen and to the clergy, who should consider Williams the worst of examples. Finally, Parson Oliver lists the ways in which *Pamela,* "a nonsensical ridiculous Book," will do harm : through its lascivious images, its instruction that young gentlemen show virtue by marrying chambermaids and that chambermaids should seek to marry their employers, its rewarding of the vile Mrs. Jewkes, and its depiction of Williams as a "good" clergyman.

With those arguments and the transcription of Shamela's papers before him, Parson Tickletext can only write back to his friend that, ashamed of the praise he had heaped on *Pamela* and angered at the presumptuous author of such an imposture, he will see to it that the "true" letters are published. And it is he who appends the information that Shamela has been thrown out of the house and that Parson Williams is being prosecuted for adultery.

THE DEDICATION

By joining *Pamela* with other works in his parody, Fielding implies that it is hardly worth burlesquing by itself — or that it

is merely illustrative of what is wrong with the widespread attitudes it embodies. The prefatory letter from " JOHN PUFF,
Esq.," for instance, though only a few sentences in length, alludes
to the author of *Pamela,* clergymen like Parson Williams, and
Robert Walpole (the Prime Minister, here called "*his Honour*"),
all of whom are accused of mistaking fashion for virtue. In Parson
Oliver's letter, criticism of *Pamela's* author includes derogatory
references to Colley Cibber and to Conyers Middleton, the latter
by means of the phrase "*Ciceronian* Eloquence."

In the same month that the second edition of *Pamela* appeared
with its adulatory testimonials, Middleton's *Life of Cicero* was
published in two sumptuous volumes, shamelessly dedicated to
Lord Hervey. This Dedication is parodied, from salutation to
signature, in the Dedication for *Shamela.* Fielding's intention is
similar to that of Alexander Pope in his "Epilogue to the Satires"
(1738), which dwells on affronts to Truth and Virtue and on the
corrupting force of Flattery. Like Fielding later, Pope drew
together Theophilus Cibber, Robert Walpole, Jonathan Wild,
Fielding's friend Lyttleton, the clergy, Hervey under the name of
"Lord Fanny," and Conyers Middleton by name and through
allusion to "that easy *Ciceronian* stile." Pope and Fielding describe flattery and false virtue as corrupting influences in every
realm of human activity. In the language of Ezra Pound, used
in connection with Ernest Hemingway's parody, *The Torrents of
Spring, Shamela* "kicks the bunk out of a number of national
imbecilities."[7]

When Middleton's *Life of Cicero* and Fielding's *Shamela* were
published, Lord Hervey had recently been elevated by Walpole
to a seat in the Cabinet as Lord Privy Seal : Vice-Chamberlain,
fop, confidant to Queen Caroline, Walpole's agent, poetaster, and
the eighteenth-century Fannius, he was an important public
figure and a familiar target for personal satire, though it never

---

[7] Ezra Pound, " Correspondence," *The New Republic,* LII (5 October,
1927), 177a.

again hit with as much genius as in Pope's "Sporus" passage in
"The Epistle to Dr. Arbuthnot" (1735). Middleton's dedication
" TO the RIGHT HONORABLE JOHN Lord HERVEY, Lord
Keeper of His Majesty's Privy Seal" is in twelve fawning paragraphs; Fielding's dedication, "To Miss *Fanny, &c.*," is in nine.
The closest of all his extended verbal parodies, and among the
funniest, the nine paragraphs of "The Dedication" are instructive
in the study of Fielding's prejudices and art. Below, the paragraphs have been set down at length alongside their source.
Middleton's "Dedication" follows on the left, Fielding's on the
right :

MY LORD,	MADAM,
The public will naturally ex-pect, that in chusing a Patron for the Life of CICERO, I should address myself to some person of illustrious rank, dis-tinguished by his parts and eloquence	It will be naturally expected, that when I write the Life of *Shamela,* I should dedicate it to some young Lady, whose Wit and Beauty might be the proper Subject of a Comparison with the Heroine of my Piece . . . .

The absurd exchange of Cicero for Shamela is followed by
logically associated exchanges of "person of illustrious rank" for
"young Lady," and "parts and eloquence" for "Wit and Beauty,"
all lowered in the direction of the trivial and frivolous.

| You see, my Lord, how much I trust to your good nature, as well as good sense, when in an *Epistle dedicatory,* the proper place of Panegyrick, I am depreciating your abilities, in-stead of extolling them : but . . . it would ill become me, in the front of such a work, to expose my veracity to any haz- | You see, Madam, I have some Value for your Good-nature, when in a Dedication, which is properly a Panegyrick, I speak against, not for you; but . . . why should I expose my Veracity to any Hazard in the Front of the Work, con-sidering what I have done in the Body. Indeed, I wish it |

ard . . . I could wish to see the dedicatory reduced to that classical simplicity, with which the ancient writers used to present their books to their friends or Patrons . . . .

was possible to write a Dedication, and get any thing by it, without one word of Flattery; but since it is not, come on . . . .

Now by omission of the phrase "good sense" Fielding implies that Hervey lacks it; by reduction of Middleton's rhetoric into "I speak against . . . you," he writes an insulting Basic English; by addition of "considering what I have done in the Body," he alludes both to Middleton's text and to his own parody of *Pamela*; and by coarse alteration of Middleton's words on dedicatory writing, he casts doubts on the "classical" high-mindedness of the flattery addressed to Hervey.

I cannot forbear boasting, that some parts of my present work have been brightened by the strokes of Your Lordship's pencil.

First, then, Madam, I must tell the World, that you have tickled up and brightened many Strokes in this Work by your Pencil.

Addition of the sensual word "tickled" to "strokes" suggests that Fielding is degrading "pencil" into an anatomical pun. One now looks back at the seemingly innocent word "Body," added to "Front," in the preceding paragraph.

It was the custom of those *Roman* Nobles, . . . in conversing with the celebrated wits and Scholars of the age . . . .

I am saying no more, my Lord, than what I know, from my constant admission to Your Lordship in my morning visits, before good manners would permit me to attempt a visit any where else; where I have found You commonly engaged with

Secondly, You have intimately conversed with me, one of the greatest Wits and Scholars of my Age.

Thirdly, You keep very good Hours, and frequently spend an useful Day before others begin to enjoy it. This I will take my Oath on; for I am admitted to your Presence in a Morning before other People's Servants are up; when I have constantly

the Classical writers of Greece or Rome. . . . for I have seen the solid effects of Your reading, in Your judicious reflections on the policy of those ancient Governments, and have felt Your weight even in controversy, on some of the most delicate parts of their History.

found you reading in good Books; and if ever I have drawn you upon me, I have always felt you very heavy.

The self-designated great scholar is now made to admit that he is merely one of Hervey's servants; and the sexual punning reaches its climax of vulgarity—punning that Middleton, by his choice of phrases, seems almost to have asked for.

I mean that singular temperance in diet, in which Your Lordship perseveres with a constancy, superior to every temptation, that can excite an appetite to rebel . . . .

Fourthly, You have a Virtue which enables you to rise early and study hard, and that is, forbearing to over-eat yourself, and this in spite of all the luscious Temptations of Puddings and Custards, exciting the Brute (as Dr. *Woodward* calls it) to rebel . . . .

An absurd subject to receive space in a book on Cicero, Hervey's control of his appetite becomes more absurd by the Dickensian naming of dishes; the bodily rebellion connected with the name of Woodward was that of vomiting, which he thought could cure most human ills ("As one of *Woodward's* Patients, sick and sore, / I puke, I nauseate,—yet he thrusts in more."— Alexander Pope, "The Fourth Satire of Dr. John Donne," ll. 152–3).

. . . personal merit : . . . after the example of your Noble Father, to open Your own way into the supreme council of the Kingdom. In this august As-

Fifthly, A Circumstance greatly to your Honour, that by means of your extraordinary Merit and Beauty; you was carried into the Ball-Room at

sembly, Your Lordship displays shining talents, . . . in the defence of our excellent Establishment; in maintaining the rights of the people, yet affecting the prerogative of the Crown; measuring them both by the equal balance of the laws . . . .

the *Bath,* by the discerning Mr. *Nash* . . . . Here you was observed in Dancing to balance your Body exactly, and to weigh every Motion with the exact and equal Measure of Time and Tune; and though you sometimes made a false Step, by leaning too much to one Side; yet every body said you would one time or other, dance perfectly well, and uprightly.

To draw a parallel, not unlike that in *Gulliver,* between dancing and maintaining political equilibrium, Fielding sets up interrelated and interacting puns. Middleton had provided "Assembly" ("Ball-Room"), "rights," "measuring," "equal," and "balance," all applicable to dancing as well as to government. Fielding's "balance," "Body," "Motion," "false Step," "leaning . . . to one Side," and "uprightly" apply even more graphically to Hervey's Cabinet than to Fanny's ball-room. After such a tissue of puns has been established, "dance perfectly well" automatically equates with "maneuver with political adroitness"; but the final phrase, "dance . . . uprightly," which can refer to a dancer's carriage or to a politician's virtuousness, reintroduces the sexual innuendo that mercilessly trails Hervey.

. . . the sprightly compositions of various kinds, with which Your Lordship has often entertained us.

. . . it was CICERO, who instructed me to write; Your Lordship, who rewards me for writing : the same motive therefore, which induced me to

Sixthly, I cannot forbear mentioning those pretty little Sonnets, and sprightly Compositions . . . .

And now, Madam, I have done with you; it only remains to pay my Acknowledgments to an Author, whose Stile I have exactly followed in this

attempt the history of the one, engages me to dedicate it to the other . . . .

Life, it being the properest for Biography. The Reader, I believe, easily guesses, I mean *Euclid's Elements*; it was *Euclid* who taught me to write. It is you, Madam, who pay me for Writing.

Fielding's *"Sixthly"* paragraph, by adding a reference to "pretty little" verses, returns to the frivolousness of the first paragraph. But the effectiveness of Euclid as a substitute for Cicero is harder to explain, although the reader is immediately surprised and amused by the exchange, sensing that *no* literary style could have been learned from Euclid's propositions and demonstrations ("Full in the midst of Euclid dip at once, / And petrify a Genius to a Dunce." — Alexander Pope, *The Dunciad*, II. 263–4). Finally the replacement of the euphemistic, ambiguous word "rewards" by the crass word "pays," which can mean nothing but "gives money," hits off in a monosyllable the relationship between patron and servant.

The name "Conny Keyber" affixed to *Shamela*'s Dedication fuses Conyers Middleton and Colley Cibber, with the additional suggestion of "cony" in the sense of "dupe," and perhaps, as Professor Watt thinks, of "cunny," Latin *cunnus*.[8] The name "Keyber" was of long standing in allusions to Cibber, as he remarks in his *Apology*: it began as a reflection on his Danish lineage.

Just as the Dedication to Miss Fanny is signed with the name of "Conny Keyber," so the title page announces: "By Mr. *CONNY KEYBER*." The funny device by which Fielding's title, *An Apology for the Life of Mrs. Shamela Andrews,* scores simultaneously against two best-sellers of 1740, *Pamela* and Cibber's *Apology,* may have been suggested by Richardson's own Preface,

---

[8] Ian Watt, *op. cit.,* p. 3.

in which he said of himself as "Editor," that "*as he is therefore confident of the favourable Reception which he boldly bespeaks for this little Work; he thinks any* further Preface *or* Apology *for it, unnecessary.*" Fielding's mock-apology grossly magnifies Richardson's "confident" editorial boldness, which was an apology for nothing, by having the more-than-confident "Editor" of *Shamela* write "to *Himself,*" that "believe me, it will go through many Editions, be translated into all Languages, read in all Nations and Ages, and to say a bold Word, it will do more good than the *C*[lerg]*y* have done harm in the World." From Richardson's first testimonial letter, too, may come another item on *Shamela's* title page; for Richardson's admirer had said that *Pamela* "will be found worthy a Place, not only in all Families . . . but in the Collections of the most curious and polite Readers." On Fielding's title page it flatly becomes "Necessary to be had in all FAMILIES."

Fielding's frisky gambados, kicking at false presentations of life and literature, are sobering as well as funny. Somewhere, between the extremes of the models and the parody, stand the accepted, unvarying terms of real life, to which the reader's thoughtful attention is directed. By means of the marvelous, negative gift of parody, showing up inconsistencies and hypocrisies, Fielding discriminates between convention and truth, pretense and action, the pretentious and the actual, the unrealities of art and artless reality. And his parody foreshadows his positive achievement of "reality" in *Joseph Andrews, Tom Jones,* and *Amelia.*

II

The Art of Comic Romance

Joseph Andrews

Now, a comic Romance is a comic Epic Poem in Prose; differing from Comedy, as the serious Epic from Tragedy: its action being more extended and comprehensive; containing a much larger Circle of Incidents, and introducing a greater variety of Characters. It differs from the serious Romance in its Fable and Action, in this; that as in the one these are grave and solemn, so in the other they are light and ridiculous: it differs in its Characters by introducing Persons of Inferiour Rank, and consequently, of inferiour Manners, whereas the grave Romance sets the highest before us: lastly, in its Sentiments and Diction; by preserving the Ludicrous instead of the Sublime.— Preface, *Joseph Andrews.*

Reading that most durable of all works of prose fiction, *Don Quixote,* we are first involved in burlesque, sharing Cervantes's critical amusement at preposterous chivalric romance, laughing at an archaic, rhetorical style; and then as we watch, the mad burlesque is wonderfully metamorphosed into "good" comic romance. After Chapter vi, as Unamuno remarks, the interest in *Don Quixote* shifts away from burlesque, from concern with words, to concern with character and society. After Quixote, lying cudgeled on the ground, is moved to declare, "I know who I am," his story alters. It becomes, says Menéndez y Pelayo, a work of

47

"purification . . . a good book of chivalry"; and Otis H. Green
feels that "Cervantes knew, as early as I, vi, that his purpose was
to write a *good* romance of chivalry," so that he wanted "to play
down the parody of the old romances and concern himself, progressively, with the problem of presenting an analysis of reality
within the framework of a book of entertainment."[1] The pattern,
exuberantly contrasting bathetic and "good" romance, is
famously effective. It is like a *burlesca* movement in music, with
brilliantly exaggerated clichés of meretricious style followed by
extended movements which rework the themes, no longer merely
cliché or parody, but something new: passionate, sympathetic,
wise, and always willing to be as ridiculous as life itself.

*The History of the Adventures of Joseph Andrews and of his
friend, Mr. Abraham Adams* (1742) opens similarly in direct
burlesque of "bad" romance, the popular romance of a letter-
writing servant girl whose virtue, in the narrow sense of physical
chastity, is rewarded by monetary gain, social elevation, and
middle-class respectability. Fielding's imitation of Cervantes, it
is always noted, appears in (1) chapter headings, (2) symbolic,
interpolated stories, (3) adventures on the road, (4) contrast of
real and illusory evils, and (5) characterization of Parson Adams.
Like Quixote, who was absorbed in a vanished world of chivalry,
Abraham Adams amusingly tries to live by the idealistic tenets of
Christianity and the Greek and Roman moralists; like Quixote
he fearlessly and thanklessly champions the oppressed and weak;
like Quixote he is "as entirely ignorant of the ways of this World
as an Infant"; and like Quixote he is an immortal figure in the
world's literature.

But, it seems to me, Fielding's announcement in his sub-title—

---

[1] Unamuno, *The Life of Don Quixote and Sancho,* trans. H. P. Earle
(New York, 1927), pp. 31–34: Menéndez y . Pelayo, cited by Ramón
Menéndez-Pidal, "The Genesis of 'Don Quixote,'" *Cervantes Across the
Centuries,* ed. Angel Flores and M. J. Benardete (New York, 1947), p. 35;
Otis H. Green, "El *Ingenioso* Hidalgo," *Hispanic Review,* XXV (July,
1957), 191.

" Written in Imitation of the *Manner* of Cervantes, Author of
Don Quixote" — may also be taken as a clue to the general structure of *Joseph Andrews*. As in *Don Quixote, a burlesca* movement
introduces themes that are, in a series of variations, elevated to a
"good" comic style. Fielding's initial burlesque of "commercial"
romance has the structural function of providing themes for the
"good" romance that follows at length. Questionable virtue,
questionably rewarded, is first burlesqued and then matched by a
vigorous depiction of true virtue, truly rewarded.[2]

BOOK I

Verbal parody, upon which the effectiveness of *Shamela* mostly
depends, seldom occurs in *Joseph Andrews*. Burlesque of situation,
while it lasts, is as funny as that in *Shamela,* though it is now
somewhat more diffused : new business, to be enlarged upon,
appears almost immediately. Parson Adams, who shares the title
of the book, is introduced in Chapter ii and is the main subject
of Chapter iii. Not active in the burlesque of *Pamela,* he signals
to the reader at the outset that other themes, rising out of the
burlesque, will follow. The initial mention of Joseph himself,
though mainly in a burlesque manner, carries at least one suggestion of an altered treatment of the story that lies ahead : " Mr.
Joseph Andrews, the Heroe of our ensuing History, was esteemed
to be the only son of Gaffar and Gammer *Andrews,* and Brother
to the illustrious *Pamela,* whose Virtue is at present so famous."
Was merely esteemed to be ! He is *not,* we finally learn, an
Andrews; he only thinks he is. When the burlesque has subsided,
Joseph turns out to be better than a male Pamela. He deserves
respect in his own right, as a man with an identity other than
that of the famous Pamela's brother, and with other things to

---

[2] I am assuming that, whatever Fielding's original plans for the scope of
Joseph Andrews may have been, he left the book as he wished it to be. If
the two opening chapters were a " false start," as they are often described,
they are not " false " to the total impact of the novel.

think about than keeping alert against an outrage on his chastity.

In two letters (I, vi, and I, x) and, when pen and ink are forbidden, in an oral apostrophe to his supposed sister (I, xiii), Joseph is made to continue the epistolary parody that set the pattern in *Shamela*, though it is now comic rather than devastating. Just as Pamela and Shamela had been pursued by (or made themselves attractive to) Mr. B. and Mr. Booby, Joseph arouses the passion of his employer, Lady Booby, Mr. B[ooby]'s aunt, recently widowed. He writes to tell how she took his hand (as Mr. B. kept taking Pamela's); and as a reminder of the hundred-or-so allusions to "virtue" in *Pamela*, he tells how he preserves his "Virtue against all Temptations." Lady Booby's overtures to him at her bedside prompt Joseph to seek an escape; so that if Pamela is "going to be married to parson *Williams,* as Folks talk," he would welcome the chance to become Williams's clerk.

Because Fielding has already dramatized for his reader Lady Booby's passionate test of Joseph, the letters and perhaps the agonized apostrophe are superfluous except as a reminder of Richardson's original epistolary fiction. The references depend for their full meaning upon the reader's familiarity with *Pamela*. Parson Williams is named here, I think, as a reminder that he would have been a far more suitable and likely mate for Pamela than would Mr. B.; in *Shamela* the role of this fellow-conspirator is of course swollen to make him Shamela's paramour and father of her child. In *Joseph Andrews* the marriage of Pamela is unknown to Joseph until late in the story (IV, v); and Joseph's reason for thinking himself a possible clerk for Parson Williams, that he can read and set a psalm, brings to mind Pamela's pride in her ability to read and in her doggerel adaptation of Psalm 137, beginning "*When sad I sat in B——n-hall,*" one of those occasions when Richardson seems to become unconsciously his own superb parodist.

I will take it as agreed that, outside of barrack-room tale-telling and Restoration comedies of wit, male chastity is not necessarily funny in itself. The Biblical Joseph ("my namesake," our Joseph writes to Pamela), aware of what the consequences may be, is heroic in his denial of Potiphar's wife. The absurdity of a squeamish male Pamela, strong, handsome, and twenty-one, is evoked by the comic setting and by the severely limited characterization that burlesque requires. When the reader laughs, it is because of Lady Booby's miscalculation of Joseph's experience in sexual matters, and then because her bid for Joseph is echoed by Mrs. Slipslop's cruder, below-stairs onslaught — in the sure-fire manner of stage comedy, where laughable antics draw forth increased laughter the second time around. The reader laughs, too, at Fielding's witty use of mock-tragic rhetoric for the passion of the employer and mock-heroic rhetoric for that of the maid. Mostly, however, the reader is entertained by Fielding's comic insights, early in the novel, into the shaky moral assumptions upon which *Pamela* was erected. Both the complexity of the state of virtue, hardly to be equated with chastity, and the general hypocrisy in sexual matters are suggested when Lady Booby recovers her speech after Joseph reproves her for inviting him into her bed: "Your Virtue! — Intolerable Confidence! . . . Will Magistrates who punish Lewdness, or Parsons who preach against it, make any scruple of committing it? And can a Boy, a Stripling, have the Confidence to talk of his Virtue?" (I, viii).

There is a point where Joseph's virtue, no longer a device for burlesque, becomes active in the story.'s "good" comic romance. Analogous with the change of mood in *Don Quixote,* the shift logically occurs in Chapter xii, when Joseph encounters two ruffians who rob him, strip him naked, and leave him lying in a ditch after beating him with sticks. This is of course like Cervantes's fourth chapter, when Don Quixote falls from his horse and is left lying on the road after two muleteers beat him and throw sticks at him; and the coach passengers who make indecent jests on Joseph's plight are like the merchants from Toledo who see in Quixote's cudgeling only an amusing anecdote to tell. This episode in Joseph's adventures, as he leaves London for the country, immediately follows the earliest notice of Fanny Goodwill, beautiful and nineteen, with whom Joseph is deeply in love. Though he had assured Lady Booby that all women were "equally indifferent to him," he had been restrained from impetuous marriage with Fanny only by the prudent advice of Parson Adams. Joseph's lack of ardor, in response to his employer's amorous proposals, becomes something other than mere prudish emulation of Pamela when we learn that, upon leaving Fanny, he had kissed her eagerly and felt high emotion when "her violent Love made her more than passive in his Embraces" (I, xi). Whereas Pamela, in her story, largely valued her chastity in order to secure economic and social security, Joseph largely values his because of his passionate devotion to his Fanny—though in the full burlesque of the earlier chapters this is unexplained and seems to be denied.

If the separation of young lovers is a romantic subject, and the romantic plots of the world's literature surely prove that it is, then the reader at this point is likely to revise his estimate of Joseph and of the evolving story itself. Convinced of handsome Joseph's unconscious ability to inflame the affections of women, one feels—through the laughter—only a kind of clinical pity for the frustrations of Lady Booby and Mrs. Slipslop, but feels some sympathy at once for the separation of the young lovers. Consequently when at Mr. Tow-wowse's inn, where Joseph is left to recover from his wounds, Betty the servant-maid indiscreetly throws herself upon him, the scene is not just a funny heightening of the episodes with Lady Booby and Mrs. Slipslop. For by this time we have learned of the charming Fanny with whom Joseph is finally to be joined and live happily ever after. The burlesque mood is past. Even Fielding's comment on Joseph's locking the door against Betty's panting entreaties—that a man should rejoice because he need not, "like a poor weak Woman," allow himself to be ravished — misses the burlesque force of other mock-sententious interpolations earlier in the novel. The scene with Betty occurs in the final chapter of Book I.

BOOK II

Although the specific burlesque of *Pamela* has now been dissipated, Joseph, Adams, and Fanny (who has thus far appeared only in Joseph's fond thoughts) must wait somewhat longer to assume full and independent characterization. The "good" romance must be earned. More than the turn of a page or two is needed to alter antic, labeled figures into heartfelt persons drawn from human nature. It can be argued that the delayed alteration is finally achieved in II, xii. Nearly half-way through the novel, this is the highly dramatic scene in which Fanny and Joseph are by good fortune brought together in the company of Parson Adams, at an ale-house inn, during a storm at night. By this time Joseph has recovered from his roadside beating, has met Adams and set out with him towards Salisbury, has been lamed by a fall from the horse he and Adams ride by turns, and has continued the journey by stage-coach and then by chaise, losing Adams along the way; in the coach he has listened to the second half of the long narrative of Leonora the Unfortunate Jilt. Adams, after hearing the first half of Leonora's tale in the coach, has fought with an innkeeper and been prankishly baptized with a panful of hog's blood, has absent-mindedly walked away from the inn without his horse, has lost his way, has rescued Fanny from a ruffian, and with her has been tried (but not convicted) because of the ruffian's perjury.

Seeking refuge from the storm, Adams and Fanny sit by the fire at the ale-house inn and hear a melodious male voice singing a love song in the Restoration pastoral mode. Like certain songs from Fielding's own comedies of ten years earlier, *The Grub-Street Opera*, for example, this one interprets a shepherd's

tormenting passion, finally gratified, in the enameled language
of "Swain" and "Nymph," "Lethe," "Narcissus," "Loves,"
"Graces," "Zephyrus," "Sweets," "Soul ... on fire," tender
"Looks," "Desire," "Madness," "Bliss," and ultimately "expiring" (in the sexual sense of Guarini's famous pun, I suppose) :

> *Advances like these made me bold;*
> *I whisper'd her,—Love, we're alone.—*
> *The rest let Immortals unfold;*
> *No language can tell but their own.*
> *Ah! Chloe, expiring, I cry'd,*
> *How long I thy Cruelty bore!*
> *Ah! Strephon, she blushing reply'd,*
> *You ne'er was so pressing before.*

It is of course the voice of Joseph which, like the sweet, musical
voice of Doña Clara's young lover in *Don Quixote*, also in an
inn at night, informs his sweetheart of his presence. We have
already been told how Joseph, as a boy, charmed even the birds
and dogs when he spoke. Recognizing her lover's voice, Fanny
says "O Jesus!" and falls back in her chair. Joseph hurries to her.
Immediately preceding the song, Fanny Goodwill has been
at length and sensually described, her sweetness a complement
to her physical perfection. Now, in what seems to be a truly
pastoral re-enactment of the song, she is ardently kissed by Joseph
and, until she recollects where she is, abandons herself to "the
Impetuosity of her Transports." A little later, with Adams
napping near them in his chair, *"Fanny*, after a thousand Entreaties, at last gave up her whole Soul to *Joseph*; and almost
fainting in his Arms, with a Sigh infinitely softer and sweeter too
than any *Arabian Breeze,* she whispered to his Lips, which were
then close to hers, 'O *Joseph,* you have won me; I will be yours
for ever.' " Fielding's rendering of emotion here is, I admit, rather
formal, but alongside the artificial, conventionalized expression
of the song, the deep-felt love of Joseph and Fanny seems like a

brilliant moment out of life itself. It is another attempt to resolve
the rivalry between the real world and the representation art
makes of it. Contrasted with the lusts of Lady Booby and Mrs.
Slipslop, the scene is a reassurance that human relationships can
offer love that is neither servile nor rancid; and contrasted with
the shadowy, unsure, and occasionally perverse emotions that
moved throughout Richardson's *Pamela,* this depiction of young
love may be said to celebrate — through comic romance — Fielding's idea of the delights and goodness in human nature.

BOOKS III–IV

After this point, II, xii, the novel importantly alters its course
and to some extent its mood. When Joseph entreats him to perform the marriage ceremony at once (lest it be after the fact!),
Parson Adams chides such enraptured haste. Joseph is admonished, as a good Christian, to wait until the third publication of
banns, so that if any person knows of impediments to the marriage, he may state them. Although Adams's contribution to the
novel as a character is vast, his place in the plot henceforth is
significantly that of a curb to the impatience of Joseph and
Fanny; in spite of threats, abductions, false charges, and Lady
Booby's displeasure, he insists upon the ritual of the banns before
he will perform the ceremony. "This Couple," he tells Lady
Booby, "were desirous to consummate long ago, and I dissuaded
them from it; nay, I may venture to say, I believe I was the sole
Cause of their delaying it" (IV, ii). Though he remains defer-
ential to Adams, Joseph deepens in character, readily asserts
himself both verbally and with his fists, and assumes leadership
in much of the action. In an interesting study entirely devoted
to Joseph's elevation in character after II, xii, Dick Taylor, Jr.,
maintains that he becomes the true hero, confident, poised, and

shrewd, expressing many of Fielding's own opinions throughout the second half of the novel.[3]

Contrasted with a prefatory burlesque romance drawing upon *Pamela* for its fun, the "good" romance, then, is the sympathetically presented love-story of Joseph and Fanny as their marriage is delayed. As in ancient romance there are mistaken identities, abduction of a beautiful maiden, feats of fisticuffs, long stories told by strangers, encounters with captious lords, Joseph's cherished talisman of a little piece of gold (never quite explained), the "sign" of identity in his strawberry mark, the gaining of a father, and tests of constancy and continence. Through encounters with fantastic dangers, unfamiliar perils, and temptations, true virtue is proved and preserved. This "good" comic romance, however, delineates the problems of lovers who are bound, not by etiquette of courtly society and obligations of their rank, but by Christian prudence and decorum.

When, for a while, it seems proved that Joseph and Fanny are brother and sister, their virtue is genuinely rewarded, far more dramatically than in most romances, or in *Pamela*; for, as Parson Adams cries out on his knees, "this Discovery had been made before the dreadful Sin of Incest was committed" (IV, xii). A better reward lies ahead; for Joseph is re-identified as the son of Mr. Wilson and is at last joined in marriage with his Fanny — "where we shall leave this happy Couple to enjoy the private Rewards of their Constancy; Rewards so great and sweet, that I apprehend *Joseph* neither envied the noblest Duke, nor *Fanny* the finest Duchess, that Night" (IV, xvi).

"Private Rewards." In thus reminding the reader of Richardson's sub-title to *Pamela*, "Or, Virtue Rewarded," I do not think Fielding can be said to revert to the burlesque with which he began his novel; nor does he do so in his final phrases, in which

---

[3] Dick Taylor, Jr., " Joseph as Hero of *Joseph Andrews*," *Tulane Studies in English*, VII (New Orleans, 1957), 91–109. Mr. Taylor's article is convincingly argued.

he announces that Joseph will not "be prevailed on by any Book-
sellers, or their Authors, to make his appearance in 'High Life,'"
perhaps referring to the anonymous imitation *Pamela in High
Life* as well as to Richardson's own sequel portraying the trials
of his heroine, as wife and mother, amongst lords and ladies.
Indeed, it occurs to me that a large part of Book IV, with which
Joseph Andrews concludes, is a kind of exercise in handling the
materials of burlesque without actually succumbing to burlesque.

Book IV opens with an account of Lady Booby and a self-
conscious reference to "this second Appearance." Pamela herself
makes an entrance with her husband, Mr. Booby, and is followed
by her parents, Gaffer and Gammer Andrews. Lady Booby's
passion for Joseph, rekindled, besides shifting the plot a little, is
now an independent study of the psychology of sexual frustration
in a mature woman. It elicits some sympathy as it certainly did
not in Book I : like the frustration of Eloisa in Pope's poem, it
turns tortuously from one emotion to another, wantonness into
self-recrimination, vindictiveness into lurid dreams, self-disgust
into crafty pretense, absurd hopes into agony. In her remarkable
soliloquy Lady Booby cries out : "What am I doing? How do I
suffer this Passion to creep imperceptibly upon me? . . . But I can
retire . . . to feed continually on Beauties, which my inflamed
Imagination sickens with eagerly gazing on; to satisfy every
Appetite, every Desire, with their utmost Wish. Ha! and do I
doat thus on a Footman? I despise, I detest my Passion.—Yet
why? Is he not generous, gentle, kind? . . . Curse his Beauties,
and the little low Heart that possesses them . . ." (IV, xiii).

Although the closing view of Pamela is that of her laughing,
to Adams's annoyance, in church, and although she is amusingly
conscious of "place," she seems to me in general quite believably
Richardson's Pamela, who has stepped out of one novel to
conduct some business in another. Her reunion with Joseph is
affectionate, she appears to be a devoted wife, and it is "with
great Decency" that she conducts herself when Fanny is pre-

sented to her as her long-lost sister and she learns that Joseph will be only a brother-in-law, not a brother. Themes, phrases, and details from Richardson's novel, like Pamela's bridal nightgown of "rich white Satin," brought to mind by Fanny's insistence upon being married in "nothing richer than a white dimity Night-Gown," are subtly appropriated into the final book of Fielding's novel; in Book I such a detail would have been pressed to stand out, for laughter's sake, in bold burlesque relief.

The nature of comic romance in prose fiction is one of the main concerns of the Preface to *Joseph Andrews,* a milestone among statements on the novel form. In his initial sentence Fielding warns his reader of an unexpected kind of entertainment in the pages ahead, for it is likely that the reader holds "a different Idea of Romance with the Author of these little Volumes." Romances like those of Mlle. de Scudéry, he says, are usually spread out through numerous volumes seriously intended, with grave action, high-born characters, and sentiments and diction meant to be sublime. A comic romance like *Joseph Andrews,* on the other hand, he says, will entertain with fable and action that are light and ridiculous, characters of low rank, and sentiments and diction intended to depict life ludicrously.

But by lightness, ridiculousness, lowness, and ludicrousness Fielding insists he does not mean to describe burlesque, but rather, life as it really is — with all its foibles and mild madnesses strongly delineated : the affectations of deceit, ostentation, and avariciousness, the vanity and hypocrisy that animate Mrs. Slipslop, Peter Pounce, Beau Didapper, passersby, and all the rest, not excluding Parson Adams nor Fanny and Joseph sometimes, and certainly not excluding the author and the reader themselves. *Joseph Andrews* does begin with burlesque, the absurd distortion of *Pamela,* exaggerating the characteristics of Lady Booby so that she represents lust alone, and exaggerating those of Joseph so that he is laughable as a prudish Adonis. When they make a reappearance, they are complex human beings rather than labeled representations. I remember the striking effect, on the stage, of Robert Ardrey's *Thunder Rock,* in which there is a similar dramatic alteration of grotesque, unsympathetic characters, the imaginary creatures of a man's mind, into complex, rounded human beings with whose emotions and experiences it is difficult not to become involved.

Hogarth, Fielding says in his Preface, is his counterpart or model in the visual arts, achieving strong character portrayal, the heightened comedy of real life, not mere caricature. Reciprocally, Hogarth engraved a plate which visually reproduces the pattern of *Joseph Andrews*'s comic romance : grotesque visages are contrasted with gatherings of "good" characterizations. In "Characters and Caricatures" (1743), Hogarth contrasts his own style as a "comic history painter" with the Italian *caricatura* manner as sometimes practised by Ghezzi, Annibal Carracci, and Leonardo, who are represented at the bottom of the plate by copies of their immense-nosed, thick-lipped, and lumpy-faced burlesques, over the word *"CARICATURAS."* Also at the bottom of the plate are three figures from Raphael, realistic cartoons identified by the word *"CHARACTERS."* The top two-thirds of the plate is fascinatingly congested with more than a hundred profiles of Hogarth's own invention, leering, simpering, grimacing, scowling, ruminating, appreciating, enduring in endless variety, all strongly presented, somewhat ridiculous, and recognizably lifelike. On his plate Hogarth has engraved, *"For a farthar Explanation of the Difference Betwixt* Character & Caricatura *See ye Preface to* Joh. Andrews."[4]

Fielding's device of fictional contrast symbolizes his attitude, in 1742, toward art and reality. The introductory, mad world of his burlesque forces the "good" world, which replaces it, to seem

[4] Mentioned in Austin Dobson, *William Hogarth,* " new and enlarged " ed. (New York and London, 1907), pp. 51, 246, and in R. E. Moore, *Hogarth's Literary Relationships* (Minneapolis, 1948), p. 113; the plate is reproduced in F. D. Klingender, *Hogarth and English Caricature* (London and New York, 1944), p. 14.

more convincing—even when that world too is nearly mad. Fielding's comic romance depicts neither idealizations nor monsters, but the entertainingly recognizable behavior of people as social beings. This romance, comic and "good," expresses a particular concept of reality by means of a challenging contrast, thus creating a world in which fiction seems truth : distorted reflections of the literary burlesque become, in the light of day, convincing images true to human nature.

"Good" comic romance, I mean to say, can achieve the illusion of reality by the display, and rejection of "bad" serious romance. " Fielding's conception of the novel as a comic epic in prose seems fundamental to the tradition he did so much to establish," says Northrop Frye. "An important theme in the more bourgeois novel should be the parody of the romance and its ideals. The tradition established by *Don Quixote* continues in a type of novel which looks at a romantic situation from its own point of view, so that the conventions of the two forms make up an ironic compound instead of a sentimental mixture. Examples range from *Northanger Abbey* to *Madame Bovary* and *Lord Jim*."[5]

In the next essay I examine a single passage from *Joseph Andrews*.

---

[5] Northrop Frye, *Anatomy of Criticism* (Princeton, 1957), p. 306.

III

The Poet and the Player

Joseph Andrews

> *"Remember," warns Epictetus in a typical passage, "that the World is a Theatre, and that your Part in this Play of Life is determined by the Poet." That is God's business. But remember, too, "that the playing of the Part assigned you, commendably, depends upon yourself. This is your Business." — Adapted by Maynard Mack.*[1]

In his fiction Fielding liked to set up a tension or establish a commentary by juxtaposing the literary and the living as counterparts. Within the total fiction of a work, the juxtaposed piece of fiction makes the presentation of "life," which is the work's main burden, more convincing. One may be an ironic counterpart of the other, as in the relationship of the formal tale of Leonora the Unfortunate Jilt to the fairly realistic story that surrounds it in *Joseph Andrews*. A good example of such an effect in a small detail is that of Parson Adams's manuscript of Aeschylus, transcribed in his own hand, flung into the fire at the ale-house inn when Fanny faints on recognizing Joseph's sweet voice. "*My Soul, whilst I gaze, is on fire: / ... Ah! Chloe, expiring, I cry'd*," Joseph sings; Fanny expires by losing consciousness; and in Fielding's words, "*AEschylus* lay expiring" in the fire. The conviction

---

[1] From Epictetus, *Encheiridion*, quoted by Maynard Mack in Introduction, Alexander Pope, *An Essay on Man*, Twickenham Ed. (London, 1950), p. xxxiv.

carried in Fielding's sympathetic account of the enraptured reunion of Fanny and Joseph partly depends upon its almost silent
relationship to the formalized sexual passion of the song (*"How
long I thy Cruelty bore!"*) and to the tragic coils of lust and
pride as they are grandly interpreted by Aeschylus. Literature
and life seem triply joined.

Joseph Andrews, III, x and xi (ix and x in 1st ed.), are a pair
of chapters which Fielding himself calls counterparts. One is
wholly literary and seemingly limited in its application, remote
from the main business of the novel; the other dramatizes a
deeply human problem involving the main characters: fiction
and life are juxtaposed for a purpose. Each chapter is in the form
of a serio-comic *agon* — a scene of verbal combat between two
speakers.

In Chapter x a Poet and a Player discourse on their art. The
stage is nowadays inferior, says the Poet, chiefly because of the
"Badness of the Actors." Not so fast, says the Player: there are
no good modern playwrights and that is what is wrong. Present
company excepted, they both politely agree. Most new plays are
terrible, the Poet now admits. Most actors would ruin a good play,
the Player subscribes, reciting from Lee's *Theodosius* and Otway's
The Orphan to prove his own excellent voice: *"Who'd be that
foolish, sordid thing, call'd Man?"* But now the Poet insists that
his own play is excellent, a very model of "Distress in a Tragedy,"
and that it was the Player's ineptitude that caused the audience
to hiss. Hissing was drawn by the play itself, says the Player,
remarking that "the Performers did the Distress of it Justice; for
I am sure we were in Distress enough, who were pelted with
Oranges all the last Act: we all imagined it would have been
the last Act of our Lives." The angry Poet is prevented from
answering him as the chapter concludes. Fielding, by providing
no answer, invites the reader to supply what is obvious, that Poet
and Player are both in part wrong, both in part right.

In the companion chapter ("a sort of Counterpart"), occurring simultaneously above-stairs, Parson Adams and Joseph engage in an impassioned dialogue while tied fast to a bedpost, facing in opposite directions. They have been secured in this symbolic relationship at the suggestion of the Poet, to prevent their rescuing Fanny, who has been cruelly abducted by a lustful Captain.

Mr. *Adams,* after many Groans, sitting with his back to *Joseph,* began thus in a sorrowful Tone : " You cannot imagine, my good Child, that I entirely blame these first Agonies of your Grief; for, when Misfortunes attack us by Surprize, it must require infinitely more Learning than you are master of to resist them; but it is the Business of a Man and a Christian to summon Reason as quickly as he can to his Aid; and she will presently teach him Patience and Submission. Be comforted, therefore, Child; I say be comforted. It is true, you have lost the prettiest, kindest, loveliest, sweetest young Woman, one with whom you might have expected to have lived in Happiness, Virtue, and Innocence; by whom you might have promised yourself many little Darlings, who would have been the Delight of your Youth and the Comfort of your Age. You have not only lost her, but have reason to fear the utmost Violence which Lust and Power can inflict upon her. Now, indeed, you may easily raise Ideas of Horror, which might drive you to Despair." — " O I shall run mad !" cries *Joseph.* " O that I could but command my Hands to tear my Eyes out and my Flesh off !" — " If you would use them to such Purposes, I am glad you can't," answered *Adams.* " I have stated your Misfortunes as strong as I possibly can; but, on the other side, you are to consider you are a Christian, that no Accident happens to us without the Divine Permission, and that it is the Duty of a Man and a Christian, to submit. We did not make ourselves; but the same Power which made us rules over us, and we are absolutely at his Disposal; he may do with us what he pleases, nor have we any Right to complain. A second Reason against our Complaint is our Ignorance; for, as we know not future Events, so neither can we tell to what Purpose any Accident tends; and that which at first threatens us with Evil may in the end produce our

Good. I should indeed have said our Ignorance is twofold (but I have not at present time to divide properly), for, as we know not to what purpose any Event is ultimately directed, so neither can we affirm from what Cause it originally sprung. You are a Man, and consequently a Sinner; and this may be a Punishment to you for your Sins : indeed in this Sense it may be esteemed as a Good, yea, as the greatest Good which satisfies the Anger of Heaven, and averts that Wrath which cannot continue without our Destruction. Thirdly, our Impotency of relieving ourselves demonstrates the Folly and Absurdity of our Complaints : for whom do we resist, or against whom do we complain, but a Power from whose Shafts no Armour can guard us, no Speed can fly? — a power which leaves us no Hope but in Submission." " O Sir!" cried *Joseph*, " all this is very true, and very fine, and I could hear you all day if I was not so grieved at Heart as now I am." " Would you take Physick," says *Adams*, " when you are well, and refuse it when you are sick? Is not Comfort to be administered to the Afflicted, and not to those who rejoice or those who are at ease?" " O! you have not spoken one Word of Comfort to me yet!" returned *Joseph*. " No!" cries *Adams*; " what am I then doing? what can I say to comfort you?" "O tell me," cried *Joseph*, " that *Fanny* will escape back to my Arms, that they shall again enclose that lovely Creature, with all her Sweetness, all her untainted Innocence about her!" " Why, perhaps you may," cries *Adams*, " but I can't promise you what's to come.[2] You must, with perfect Resignation, wait the Event : if she be restored to you again, it is your Duty to be thankful, and it is if she be not. *Joseph*, if you are wise and truly know your own Interest, you will peaceably and quietly submit to all the Dispensations of Providence, being thoroughly assured that all the Misfortunes, how great soever, which happen to the Righteous, happen to them for their own Good. Nay, it is not your Interest only, but your Duty, to abstain from immoderate Grief; which if you indulge, you are not worthy the Name of a Christian." He spoke these last words with an accent

---

[2] The 1st ed. has only: " . . . what's to come. The Doctrine I teach you is a certain Security—nay, it is not your Interest only, but your Duty . . . ." Thus two sentences are interpolated in the 2nd ed., on which my text is based.

a little severer than usual; upon which *Joseph* begged him not to
be angry, saying, he mistook him if he thought he denied it was
his Duty, for he had known that long ago. " What signifies knowing
your Duty, if you do not perform it?" answered *Adams*. " Your
Knowledge increases your guilt. O *Joseph*! I never thought you
had this Stubborness in your Mind." *Joseph* replied, he fancied he
misunderstood him; " which I assure you," says he, " you do, if
you imagine I endeavour to grieve : upon my soul I don't." *Adams*
rebuked him for swearing, and then proceeded to enlarge on the
Folly of Grief, telling him, all the wise Men and Philosophers, even
among the Heathens, had written against it, quoting several passages
from *Seneca,* and the " Consolation," which, though it was not
Cicero's, was, he said, as good almost as any of his Works; and
concluded all by hinting that immoderate Grief in this Case might
incense that Power which alone could restore him his *Fanny.* This
Reason, or indeed rather the Idea which it raised of the Restoration
of his Mistress, had more effect than all which the Parson had said
before, and for a moment abated his Agonies; but, when his Fears
sufficiently set before his Eyes the Danger that poor Creature was
in, his Grief returned again with repeated Violence, nor could
Adams in the least asswage it; though it may be doubted in his
Behalf whether *Socrates* himself could have prevailed any better.

They remained some time in silence, and Groans and Sighs issued
from them both; at length *Joseph* burst out into the following
Soliloquy : —

> *" Yes, I will bear my Sorrows like a Man,*
> *But I must also feel them as a Man.*
> *I cannot but remember such things were,*
> *And were most dear to me."*

Adams asked him what Stuff that was he repeated? To which he
answered, they were some Lines he had gotten by heart out of a
Play. " Aye, there is nothing but heathenism to be learned from
Plays," reply'd he. " I never heard of any plays fit for a Christian to
read, but *Cato* and the *Conscious Lovers;* and, I must own, in the
latter there are some things almost solemn enough for a Sermon."

Fielding's manipulation of this passage is highly effective, as in his comic underplaying of a detail like "*Adams* rebuked him for swearing, and then proceeded to enlarge on the Folly of Grief." "They remained some time in silence," followed by Joseph's impassioned application of Macduff's lines[3] to his own situation, is strongly felt, rising above its context of comic romance. Never intruding as "author," Fielding is in perfect control of matter and manner. As the man of God, Parson Adams represents the Poet, maintaining that our part in this play of life is already determined. Life may seem dreadful, he says, but it seems so because of the actions of men. Joseph, held helplessly fast to the bedpost, tormented by the thought of Fanny's violation by the Captain, cannot reasonably resign himself, but groans and says he would, like a hero in a Greek tragedy, tear off his flesh to show his despair. As the Player in the theater of life he tries to do his best with the part assigned him, but the Poet perhaps expects too much. The situation, Poet-Parson admits, could hardly be more discouraging, yet it is the reasonable duty of ignorant Man to submit to the large design. Ordinarily, Player-Joseph agrees, reason should be followed, but on this occasion his heart commands him. Poet-Parson becomes more severe, admonishing him as a Christian to abstain from immoderate grief. Player-Joseph stubbornly insists it is impossible for him to subdue his feelings; he borrows Shakespeare's language to express himself. Most plays are unChristian, Poet-Parson objects, leaving their dialogue, like that of the Poet and Player below-stairs, unresolved.

Joseph and Adams are sympathetically presented in an absurd situation, laughable if one envisions two notably brawny men tied facing in opposite directions, to represent their opposing views of life. Fielding contrasts the suffering and consolation of these two virtuous men with the "literary" or affected suffering and consolation of the two vain men whose petty discourse he sets forth in the companion chapter. Though their "sorrows" are

[3] William Shakespeare, *Macbeth*. IV, iii, 219–222.

due to pretensions and inadequacies of imagination, the ego-centric Player and Poet of Chapter x blame each other for their failures. Indifferent to the misfortunes of others, as they had indifferently stood by while Fanny was carried off, the Player and Poet are meanly ridiculous, lacking in the qualities they attempt to magnify.

Although Adams and Joseph have none of the meanness of the Poet and Player, they are also ridiculous in this episode. Like the Poet, Adams falls here into the error of adopting an extreme in order to correct another. In his impromptu sermon exhorting Joseph to reason and resignation, Adams introduces his arguments abominably in highly colored pictures of Fanny's attractions and of her possible rape—appealing to exactly those emotions he says he wants Joseph to control. Like the Poet below-stairs, too, he paradoxically shifts and varies his approach to the subject under consideration. He offers three reasons why Joseph must submit, erected on the overall premise that Providence rules the world : (1) nothing happens without divine assent; (2) this may ultimately be a good; and (3) we are impotent to help ourselves. First he is doctrinaire, but Joseph will have none of his advice. Then he is philosophical. Then he is again theologically doctrinaire, resting his confidence on his faith and on the ordered reasonableness he thinks he possesses. Finally he quotes classical precedent for considering grief a folly. He lacks imagination to know how he will conduct himself when his own heart is taken by surprise.

The completely innocent Joseph, who has done nothing to pull down sorrow upon himself, faces what seems to him real misfortune, and his distress touches the human heart when he blurts out his simple plea for Fanny's safe, untainted return. Though undignified, his sorrow is affecting. But the sense of detail betrays him when, after he has first listened to Adams, he allows himself to display his grief immoderately. When he cries that he would tear out his eyes and rip off his flesh if he had use of his hands, he does not stop to think that with his hands he could be engaged more practically in saving Fanny. His melodramatic outcries are reminiscent in tone and vocabulary of speeches in heroic tragedies which Fielding had satirized in *Tom Thumb* and elsewhere. Guilty of affectation, since his uncontrolled state of grief, like the Player's indignation, amounts to play-acting, Joseph is somewhat ridiculous.

In his quotation from *Macbeth* Joseph reveals that although he values reason in the face of sorrows, still " *I must also feel them as a Man.*" "Heart" means much to Joseph, essentially a man of feeling, whose use of the word in his last speech in the chapter carries a double meaning when he says in reply to Adams's question that the lines from Shakespeare are "some Lines he had gotten by heart out of a Play." Joseph wants to join Shakespeare in expressing the sublimity of terror : the terror here is in the abduction of Fanny and the "horror" that Joseph imagines may follow. But the quotation is taken from Macduff's dialogue with Malcolm after Macbeth causes Macduff's wife and children to be slaughtered in a most horrible act of bloody violence. If we compare Macduff's loss to that of Joseph, the whole structure of "sublimity" crumbles. There is sublimity in Macduff's words in their proper context, but here the danger to Fanny is only ridiculously imagined by Joseph; she is quite unharmed after all.

But by associating himself with Shakespeare, Joseph dignifies himself above Adams, who dismisses the quotation as "Stuff" and advertises that Addison's *Cato* and Steele's *The Conscious Lovers* are the only plays he knows of "fit for a Christian to read." In his rejecting *Macbeth* for these plays, Adams's reasonableness breaks down to judgment by taste—here a choice for mere posturing, impossible virtues, and false emotionalism masquerading as noble feeling. Thus, after his sermonizing on one's duty as a man and as a Christian, Adams approves of sentimental fare which mocks at moral values and promotes the idea that evil and injustice can be washed away with tears. False sentiment is constantly one of the targets for Fielding's wit. The code of behavior based on benevolism, reason, and control is commendable for society, and to some extent Fielding's century felt that this code had saved society from the dissolution of culture threatened by the Puritan Revolution. As a code for the conduct of the individual it is less useful; for despite the basic assumptions of an age, human nature remains constant—usually imprecise and muddled, needing control, decorum, and discipline, but overpowered when the passions assume command. There is a discrepancy between the reasonable code of conduct (Adams, Addison, Steele) and the psychological organization of man (Joseph, Shakespeare, Fielding). Essentially the moral sentiments of Addison and Steele are alien to Adams's basic goodness, and are for him a form of affectation, like his attempts at false learning in quoting from Seneca and Boethius to establish a point in argument. Fielding's ironic comment on Joseph's "Tears, which would have become any but a Heroe," directly opposes Steele's philosophy, that a sentimental tear is preferable to vulgar laughter. Fielding himself is having serious fun, it seems to me, with Adams, Joseph, Addison, Steele, and the reader. Joseph is no hero : he *is* a man.

This dramatic dialogue between the Parson and Joseph, the one advocating rational submission to Providence and the other basically representing human nature, is refereed by an invisible third character, as in the dialogue of the Poet and Player also, who makes his presence felt, standing apart from these two fictitious characters, and who, drawing upon his knowledge of life as it must be lived, implies the middle way between them. This technique presents an essential idea of Fielding, that a humorous, good-natured, common-sense approach to life is the best aim of man : humorous, because laughter is an instrument of truth, routing out excess, which is ridiculous. In the *Essay on Man* Pope's rhymes show how man's passions urge him on and how his reason controls him; how, in other words, man must be

seen from the point of view of both Poet and Player, both Adams
and Joseph. Man is contemptible, admirable, and — in the pages
of *Joseph Andrews* — nearly always amusing. Fielding seems to
affirm that the true Christian concept of man is tough enough to
meet and include both reason and emotion; both Houyhnhnm
and Yahoo, Swift would have said. The Christian and classical
precepts of Adams are inadequate for Joseph's comfort. But we
laugh at Joseph's distress; for in a comic romance it is unlikely
that the heroine will be violated or killed.

Fielding commits himself on the proper place of emotions when
Joseph is released from the bedpost, Fanny is recovered, and the
lovers are reunited : " O Reader ! conceive if thou canst the Joy
which fired the Breasts of these Lovers on this Meeting; and if thy
own Heart doth not sympathetically assist thee in this Conception,
I pity thee sincerely from my own; for let the hard-hearted
Villain know this, that there is a Pleasure in a tender Sensation
beyond any which he is capable of tasting" (III, xii). Further, in
the year after publication of *Joseph Andrews,* Fielding committed himself on the relationship of emotion and reasonable
fortitude. Can a good man summon reason immediately in the
event of disaster? No : he will first be moved by strong feeling :
" And here I address myself to common Men, and who partake
of the more amiable Weaknesses of Human Nature . . . . Nay, I
shall not regard Tears, Lamentation, or any other Indulgence to
the first Agonies of our Grief on so dreadful an Occasion,
as Marks of Effeminacy; but shall rather esteem them as the
Symptoms of a laudable Tenderness, than of a contemptible
Imbecility of Heart. . . . The Mind of a wise Man may be
ruffled and discolored, but cannot be subdued . . . . With whatever
Violence our Passions at first attack us, they will in Time subside.
It is then that Reason is to be called to our Assistance, and we
should use every Suggestion which it can lend to our Relief . . ."
("Of the Remedy of Affliction for the Loss of Our Friends,"
Miscellanies, 1743, I, 306–308). Fortitude, celebrated as a leading

virtue by ancient moralists and primitive Christians alike, does not require a disposition callously resigned in the midst of human calamity : *"Yes, I will bear my Sorrows like a Man, / But I must also feel them as a Man."*

In the total structure of *Joseph Andrews,* Parson Adams's bedpost-harangue on the "Duty, to abstain from immoderate Grief" is an ironic preparation for the inevitable later episode when the Parson too will display tears rather than fortitude. It is, of course, the famous episode of the "drowning" of Adams's son Jacky (IV, viii), with which my next essay is for the most part concerned.

IV

A Comic Mythology

Joseph Andrews

*I see your hearts affected, I see your eyes weep. (And
indeed, who can refrain weeping at the relation of such a
story?) But, behold, I show you a mystery, hid under the
sacrifice of* Abraham's *only son, which, unless your hearts
are hardened, must cause you to weep tears of love, and
that plentifully too.—George Whitefield.*[1]

E. M. Forster remarks in passing that in *Joseph Andrews*
"Fielding set out to use *Pamela* as a comic mythology."[2] That is
true in the sense that in 1742 *Pamela* had popularly assumed the
guise of ritual, so that Virtue could be partially evoked and
possibly Rewarded in the sheer act of reading through Richardson's pages. Readers, especially feminine readers under Richardson's full and powerful spell, perhaps thought they could get
what they wanted by reading about it, by day-dreaming that they
had it. This is one of the attractions of such a novel. The extravagant insistence upon the moral powers of *Pamela* in its title-page,
preface, and testimonial letters (all of which Fielding had turned
inside out in *Shamela*) seems to enforce the idea that virtue could
be especially accessible after one had read that novel. Persons
who might have drawn their day-dreams from Biblical stories
and their own experiences could find new matter for dreams and

---

[1] George Whitefield, Sermon III, "*Abraham's* offering up his Son *Isaac*,"
Works (London, 1772), V, 47.
[2] E. M. Forster, *Aspects of the Novel* (New York, 1927), p. 175.

imitation in the story of Pamela, who, after a series of trials to
prove her fitness, gained happiness and plenty through the public
ceremony of marriage, creating for herself a seemingly perfect
world. The story had been ritually read out to the female mem-
bers of Richardson's family in installments as he wrote it; and it
is said that in Slough the local blacksmith read out the story
serially to the villagers, who celebrated Pamela's accomplishment
of marriage to Mr. B. by ringing the church bells.[3] Fielding's
creation of a supposed brother for Pamela of course extends this
brand-new, popular myth, but does so in terms of comedy, with
characters, episodes, and language all spiced with ridicule.

But Joseph is not only Pamela's supposed brother; at the outset
he is introduced as an amusing modernization of the Old Testament Joseph (:"my namesake"). Like the Biblical Joseph he ex-
emplifies patience and chastity; like the Biblical Joseph he is a
"goodly person, and well-favoured." He has been kidnapped by
gipsies (Egyptians), and has been employed in a great house, has
rejected the sexual advances of his master's wife, and has suffered
from her resulting fury. He is finally revealed in his true identity,
is reconciled with his family, and weeps while embracing his
father from whom he has been so long separated. Part of the
effect of *Joseph Andrews* comes from Fielding's borrowing the
portentous Old Testament myth and altering it comically with
Potiphar's wife now as Lady Booby, Jacob as Mr. Wilson. And
Biblical phrasing is absorbed into Fielding's story : it is not at
first sight, I think, easy to say which Joseph is being reconciled
with his father if the following is read out of context : " he threw
himself at his Feet, and, embracing his Knees with tears begged
his Blessing."

Our Joseph has achieved his status as exemplar and pattern of
virtue by heeding Parson Abraham Adams's "many Admon-
itions concerning the Regulation of his future Conduct, and his
Perseverance in Innocence and Industry" (I, iii). Adams, who

---

[3] Wilbur L. Cross, *The History of Henry Fielding* (New Haven, 1918),
I, 303.

derives not at all from *Pamela* (except possibly as a corrective to Parson Williams), pushes comic myth to perfection. He is "the old Adam," Adam the father of mankind, and Abraham the father of the faithful, guided by an intense faith in God which supports him, with one or two slips. Like his Biblical prototype our Abraham passes through hostile and corrupt lands to reach his true home, and he passes through unscathed. As Joseph's spiritual adviser he represents moral order in the novel. "Abraham shall surely become a great and mighty nation, and all the nations of the earth shall be blessed in him."[4]

As a dedicated clergyman Adams is the spiritual center for his society. The displacement of Christian feeling in that society is made evident again and again in the treatment he suffers outside his church: he is laughed at, maligned, physically bruised, confined, dismissed, humiliated, and repeatedly made a butt for abuse. The manners and morals of the company of persons Adams meets, from high life and low, are tested in how they treat him. He is generally a subject for laughter, and the reader is forced to join in the laughter at Adams's expense — although by means of Fielding's art the reader feels sympathy and respect for goodness through the laughter.[5]

In his church and with his surplice on, however, Adams is not a source for laughter. A man of "true Christian Piety," he publicly rebukes Pamela and her husband on the occasion of Joseph's

---

[4] Genesis XVIII: 18.

[5] "One might conjecture that through Adams Fielding intended to demonstrate that virtue cannot be made ridiculous. Exposure to affectation is necessarily censorious and negative."—W. R. Irwin, " Satire and Comedy in the Works of Henry Fielding," *ELH* (September, 1946), 185–186. Of course exposure is censorious, but it is not necessarily damning. Like many commentators Mr. Irwin does not give Fielding credit for creating a complex character in Adams. Mark Spilka, using the mix-up of beds in Booby Hall as his main illustration, argues that Fielding intentionally shows Adams in comic and "naked" situations in order to resolve the major themes of the novel through benevolent humor and through insistence that people must be accepted sympathetically for what they really are.—" Comic Resolution in Fielding's *Joseph Andrews*," *College English*, XV (October, 1953), 11–19,

wedding, for unsuitable behavior "in so sacred a Place, and on so solemn an Occasion" :

Our Parson would have done no less to the highest Prince on Earth; for, though he paid all Submission and Deference to his Superiours in other Matters, where the least Spice of Religion intervened he immediately lost all Respect of Persons. It was his Maxim, that he was a Servant of the Highest, and could not, without departing from his Duty, give up the least Article of his Honour or of his Cause to the greatest earthly Potentate. Indeed, he always asserted that Mr. *Adams* at Church with his Surplice on, and Mr. *Adams* without that Ornament in any other place, were two very different Persons. (IV, xvi)

Much of the greatness of Adams's conception and of his contribution to the novel lies in his being "two very different Persons." He is, first, the scapegoat enduring the cruelties and slapstick indignities of a society organized in terms of caste and money-power, though he shakes his crabstick against them; and, second, wearing the vestments of office in his Father's house, he is absolutely in control, performing sacred rites, reproving folly, and dispensing justice among his social superiors. The second Parson Abraham Adams extends outside the comic boundaries of the novel : Fielding does not allow him to be seen in his surplice until the comic complications of the novel have been resolved.

In the opinion of M. C. Battestin, Fielding's use of Biblical analogues for Abraham Adams, and for Joseph Andrews as well, was influenced by published sermons on the themes of charity and the "man of good nature." "The true origin of Fielding's twin protagonists in their capacity as moral exemplars in this low-life epic of the road may be traced with confidence to the homilies, and in particular, it would seem, to Isaac Barrow's sermon 'Of Being Imitators of Christ.' "[6] In that sermon Barrow

---

[6] M. C. Battestin, *The Moral Basis of Fielding's Art: A Study of " Joseph Andrews "* (Middletown, Conn., 1959), p. 26.

had recommended the examples of the Scriptural Abraham (pattern of true faith) and the Scriptural Joseph (model of chastity); both are "illustrious patterns of virtue and piety." Mr. Battestin quotes appropriate passages from sermons by Barrow, Clarke, South, and Hoadly—divines with whose religious tenets Fielding generally felt strong agreement.[7] But it seems to me possible that Fielding's comic Biblical mythology may equally stem from sermons by divines like Whitefield, with whom he was generally in disagreement. In my epigraph to this chapter I quote a specimen of insidious, sly, sentimental rhetoric from Whitefield's sermon on "*Abraham's* offering up his Son *Isaac.*" It could inspire comedy.

Abraham Adams must have thought he was like the "wise Man" who "cooly answered the Person who acquainted him with the Death of his Son—I KNEW *I had begot a Mortal*" ("Of the Remedy of Affliction for the Loss of Our Friends," *Miscellanies,* 1743, I, 305). When tested, however, he did *not* care to offer up his son Jacky, "the sweetest, best-temper'd Boy, who never did a thing to offend me." The episode of Jacky's "drowning," one of the best-constructed scenes in Fielding's repertory, is the most arresting Biblical analogue in *Joseph Andrews* (IV, viii). It closely follows Genesis XXII : 1–18, though with comic (and human) differences. "And it came to pass after these things that God did tempt Abraham, and said unto him, 'Abraham : and he said, 'Behold, here I am.' " The unquestioning faith of both Abrahams is tested; they are both tempted by what seem to be the deaths of their young sons, the darlings and comforts of their old age. As Erich Auerbach expresses it in his remarkable analysis of the Biblical episode, "God gives his command in direct discourse, but he leaves his motives and his purpose unexpressed; Abraham, receiving the command, says nothing and does what he has been told to do." Auerbach shows that beyond the naming of objects and actions, "time and place are undefined and call for

---

[7] *Ibid.,* pp. 26–43, 85–103.

interpretation; thoughts and feeling remain unexpressed . . . ."[8]

It is quite otherwise in Fielding's amusing adaptation. Adams is again sermonizing for Joseph's edification, this time on the subject of the young man's eagerness to make Fanny his wife. If carnal impatience is the motive, Adams says, then Joseph is guilty of sin; if fears concerning Fanny's well-being are the motive, then Joseph must learn to put his trust in divine Providence. He must learn to submit in all things, must be able to resign himself "peaceably, quietly, and contentedly" even to the loss of his love. "At which Words one came hastily in, and acquainted Mr. *Adams* that his youngest Son was drowned." Showing no Christian fortitude or trust in the will of Providence, Adams is at first stunned; then he stamps about; then he unrestrainedly bewails his loss, "lamenting, whilst the Tears trickled down into his Bosom." When Jacky himself appears, wet but undrowned, and his father resumes his admonitory remarks to Joseph on the control of passions, Joseph for the first time asserts himself strongly in rebellion. Earlier, tied to the bedpost, he had received Adams's Cato-like advice respectfully, but now he interrupts to say that it is "easier to give Advice than to take it" and that Adams's own actions are at odds with his advice. Annoyed at seeing his authority slip away, Adams raises his voice to call Joseph an ignorant boy who cannot comprehend his fatherly tenderness for Jacky. When Joseph, still defiant, makes an analogy of his tender feelings for Fanny, Adams terms such love a foolish matter of the flesh and warns that married love should be governed by "Moderation and Discretion." Then, says Joseph, he will have to reconcile himself to sinning, for he does not intend to observe moderation in his love for Fanny. At this point a referee, in the person of Mrs. Adams, decides that the parson's counsel and practice are inconsistent. "Don't hearken to him, Mr. *Joseph*," she recommends as Fielding's spokesman.

---

[8] Erich Auerbach, *Mimesis,* trans. Willard Trask (Princeton, 1953), pp. 8–11.

Yet to whom must we hearken, if not to Abraham the patriarch and archetype of charity and good nature? What is Fielding's intention, beyond providing amusement, when he shows his Parson's flawed, all-too-human nature? It may be true, as Mr. Battestin says, that "Adams's inability to follow his own advice on this occasion only sharpens our awareness of his compassionate nature."[9] But the real significance of the episode comes clear when we reach, a few pages later, Adams's true evaluation of himself as "two very different Persons," "at Church with his Surplice on" and "without that Ornament, in any other place."

In the episode involving Jacky we have seen Adams guilty of a breach of decorum; for when he is tested, he has been presumptuously acting in a domestic situation as though he stood in his pulpit wearing his surplice. James Sutherland puts it neatly : " What lies behind the episode is partly Fielding's perception (which he shared with Swift) of the way in which a man's profession is apt to become the man himself . . . . In his lengthy homily to Joseph, the parson has been behaving professionally, using the jargon of his profession, inculcating principles which are probably impracticable, and which in any case he cannot live up to himself. And then Fielding shows us the real man." The laughter called up by that revelation is directed less at Adams than toward those persons "who suppose that the goodness inculcated by preaching and virtuous maxims is ever likely to stand up to the test of real life."[10] The "Test of Real Life," it seems to me, is what Fielding selected for his theme when he announced his concern with "the true Ridiculous" in his Preface to *Joseph Andrews*.

The episode concerning Jacky could in its entirety withstand — and perhaps would profit from — the dredging up of verbal effects to which I have earlier subjected *Shamela*. But most of the allu-

---

[9] M. C. Battestin, *op. cit.*, p. 109.
[10] James Sutherland, *English Satire* (Cambridge, England, 1958), pp. 114–115.

sions and adaptations, such as echoes from the Poet-and-Player scene and from the bedpost scene, operate within *Joseph Andrews* itself. I want, however, to look more closely at two sentences from the episode. The first, a part of Adams's harangue for Joseph's benefit, follows directly after the statement that "All Passions are criminal in their Excess, and even Love itself, if it is not subservient to our Duty, may render us blind to it":

"Had *Abraham* so loved his Son *Isaac* as to refuse the Sacrifice required, is there any of us who would not condemn him?"

With that sentence the rhythm and phrasing abruptly alter from the sound of eighteenth-century homilies to that of the King James Version—especially to the sound of "For God so loved the world, that he gave his only begotten Son." Scriptural mythology has provided two archetypal tests of fathers willing to sacrifice their sons, both Old and New Testament examples suggestively conjoined in Parson Adams's question to Joseph. As ironic preparation for what is to follow, and to enforce the analogue from the Bible, Fielding causes Abraham Adams to name his prototype and, through the reference to Isaac, sets the scene for Jacky. Adams's harsh (un-Christian?) rhetoric in "is there any of us who would not condemn him?" rushes headlong toward the answer of "Yes, we would not condemn him." Adams unwisely asks for condemnation which will ironically involve him a minute later:

At which Words one came hastily in, and acquainted Mr. *Adams* that his youngest Son was drowned.

This second remarkable sentence follows directly after Adams's rather unctuous insistence upon the duty of quiet resignation to divine Providence. Although it has been prepared for (as the reader sees in looking a little way. back), the sentence comes as a shock. It is oddly divided, beginning with Biblical phrasing and then turning to flat, cold-blooded journalistic statement of fact. In an English novel of any period we would expect to read, "At which Words a limping pedlar came hastily in," or "At which Words Mr. Bumble, his eyes staring, came hastily in." Fielding has purposely begun the sentence in the Scriptural style that Erich Auerbach called "unexpressed," loftily not bothering with non-essentials. Parson Adams at home still imagines himself in the role of the Poet, the Father, patriarchal Abraham, the Pastor in his surplice. But with the domestic, heart-rending news, terrible to a human father, with which the sentence concludes, the Biblical analogue goes up in smoke.

Divine excellence and human defect are joined in Parson Adams. *"As to the Character of Adams,"* Fielding wrote in his Preface, *"as it is the most glaring in the whole, so I conceive it is not to be found in any Book now extant."* The word *glaring* catches one's attention. Is it the glaring discrepancy between "Father Abraham" and "the old Adam" that renders the Parson somewhat ridiculous? Not long after the publication of *Joseph Andrews* there appeared a definition of ridicule more sharply phrased than Fielding's own, and capable of applying to Adams as Fielding's does only uneasily, and with *glaring* as one of its key words:

RIDICULE *is a free* Attack *of any* Motly Composition, *wherein a real or affected* Excellence *and* Defect *both jointly appear,* glaring *together, and* mocking *each other, in the same* Subject.[11]

Ridicule in this sense can hardly apply to Lady Booby, Mrs. Slipslop, Beau Didapper, or Parson Trulliber, whose over-spreading defects make their excellences undiscernible, nor is it appropriate to Joseph and Fanny, whose goodness predominates throughout most of the novel. But in Adams, for whom the reader feels interest and affection not shared by any of the other char-acters, excellence and defect do indeed mock and glare together. Fielding's friendly, artful, *"free* Attack" renders Adams ridic-

---

[11] Corbyn Morris, *An Essay Towards Fixing the True Standards of Wit, Humour, Raillery, Satire, and Ridicule* (London, 1744), p. 36.

ulously great. And this kind of "Attack" will contribute to Fielding's presentation of the greatly conceived, glaring characters of Tom Jones and Billy Booth.

V

The Art of the Novel

Tom Jones

A few of the essays in Tom Jones *do deserve cold looks,
but in most of them he makes a very fair business of
writing an equivalent to Aristotle's* Poetics *for the novel.
— Rebecca West.*[1]

An Epistle to the Reader; why?—Anthony Scoloker.[2]

Although the preface to a novel may itself be feigning, it is
usually intended to let the author speak for himself, preparatory
to his conducting his reader out of the "real" world into the
feigned world of his fiction. In *Tom Jones* Fielding not only
writes a preface—or, rather, eighteen prefaces—but calls his
reader's attention to the act, first in his introductory "Bill of
Fare" and then in what he´ variously alludes to as "initial
Essays," "digressive Essays," and "prefatory Chapters," on
which he says he has lavished special care. Cervantes, a fore-
runner in this as one might guess, had whimsically assured his
reader that "I have found no task more difficult than the composition of this preface you are now reading."[3]

Self-conscious prefaces, which discuss their own identities, did

---

[1] Rebecca West, *The Court and the Castle* (New Haven, 1957), p. 104.

[2] Anthony Scoloker, Preface, *Daiphantus* (1604), quoted in *An Anthology
of Elizabethan Dedications & Prefaces,* ed. Clara Gebert (Philadelphia,
1933), p. 154.

[3] Cervantes, Prologue, Part I, *Don Quixote.*

not, of course, originate with Fielding's novels. In 1655, almost a hundred years before *Tom Jones*, Roger Boyle, Lord Broghill, treated his introductory remarks to *Parthenissa: A Romance* as a novelty by saying that "Though a Preface before a booke of this Nature is seldome writt, and seldomer Read," yet he is proffering one — and is in the very act of penning it. Congreve's preface to *Incognita* (1692), however, pleads convention rather than novelty and, making some significant critical statements along the way, pretends wearily to gratify the bookseller by padding. In his ironic guise of "the *freshest Modern*," Swift announces to readers of *A Tale of a Tub* (1704) that he will forgo personal anecdote which would swell the size of "this Preface into the Size now in Vogue." Again, making convention his excuse for introductory remarks to a work of fiction, Defoe says that "Prefaces are so customary before Books of this Nature, to introduce them into the World by a Display of their Excellencies, that it might be thought too presuming to send this Performance abroad, without some such Preliminary" (*Colonel Jack*, 1722).

By the time *The History of Tom Jones, A Foundling* (1749), was published, then, prefaces were not only conventional and expected, but often a chore to write and a bore to read. A preface to a novel might be characterized as a porch leading to the main edifice; a bow before entering the drawing-room; a polite chat at the gate of Entertainment and Instruction; or a kind of intellectual "something short" before the start of a journey; but authors admitted (or sometimes pretended) that this "something short" was only a way of satisfying the publisher, another tiresome convention attendant on authorship. Nothing new in themselves, Fielding's prefaces in *Tom Jones* are different from others in two general ways : they are the lively work of unquestionable genius; and they are numerous!

The success of *Tom Jones* among readers may be judged in part by its almost immediate conversion into a model for other novels. Whereas *Pamela* at first invited parodies, *Tom Jones*

⟨encouraged imitations. Some of these are *The History of Char-⟩
lotte Summers (1750), *The History of Pompey the Little* (1751),
The Adventures of Captain Greenland (1752), *The Placid Man*
(1770), and—to jump on ahead in time—*Henry* (1795). *Charlotte Summers* boasts that here is "the first Begotten, of the
poetical Issue, of the much celebrated Biographer of *Joseph
Andrews,* and *Tom Jones*"; its four book-divisions possess imi-
tative introductory essays. *Captain Greenland,* signed with the
name "William Goodall," prefaces nine of its twelve books with
discursive essays, some of them in mock distress complaining that
"it somewhat strains us to find out Matter prefatory to each
Book" (III, i). But although prefaces must be eked out, because
"the great Mr. F–ld–g seems to have set it down for a Rule,"
this author has "in several Places, already, thought it full as
proper to set that Rule at naught" (XII, i). Announcing his imitation of the "ingenious Mr. Henry Fielding" in *The Placid Man,*
Charles Jenner addresses the reader to introduce his six book-
divisions, twice in verse form. Almost at the close of the century
Richard Cumberland's *Henry* introduces every one of its twelve
books with "short prefatory Essays [devoted] to our fraternity of
Novelists" (VI, i). These prefaces, we are told, serve, like Fielding's, as places of refreshment, roadside inns, or "baiting-places."
Fielding's idea that a writer's intellect and judgment can be tested
in his prefaces is borne out in works like *The Rencontre,* by a Lady
(1785), who confides, "My bookseller, gentle Reader, wants me to
write a preface; but to what purpose?" A silly preface flashes
signals that more silliness lies ahead in efforts like *Mentoria* (1791),
by Mrs. Rawson, who apologizes that "though I have taken up
my pen to write a preface, I am utterly at a loss what to say."

In his Preface to *Joseph Andrews,* Fielding had tried, first by
analogy and distinctions, to settle both the scope and mode for
the new prose fiction of which he was self-consciously the inno-
vator; and then he had tried, radically, to hit off its subject
matter in a single word. His comic prose epic, differing from

narrative poetry as well as from serious prose romance, was to lay out the "ridiculous," which Shaftesbury had dignified as a "test of truth," and by which Fielding probably meant the rendering of characters and their actions in a manner heightened but faithful to human nature, never brushing off the absurdities, big and little, that speckle even a hero, if he is human.

Although these defining themes recur in the critical prefaces to the eighteen books of *Tom Jones,* Fielding now proceeds (1) to establish qualifications "in a pretty high Degree necessary" to future authors of works like *Tom Jones*; (2) to elucidate the craft of fiction under several headings; and (3) to plead for the reader's attention and appreciation in matters both aesthetic and moral. Under each of these three headings he proffers lucid examples to make his meaning certain. Like the founder of a newly-opened country, he assumes the responsibility for laying down interim laws to govern this new province of writing. And because the province is a comic one, as well as because it is Fielding who does the critical legislating, these laws, speculations, and confidences are set down amusingly. The light touches, raillery, grotesque metaphors, mock rodomantade, manly humor, and "ludicrous Observations," as he calls them, are intended not merely to amuse but to draw the serious reader into consideration of specialized critical matters. Fielding says that he hopes to reach as wide an audience as possible, and that all his wit and humor are spread out to please his "Customers," but that he will bid a quick farewell to those readers who are unable or unwilling to exert their keenest powers of judgment and penetration. When he shares his pioneering discoveries, he is reaching out a long way, we now know, to novelists as like or unlike himself as Jane Austen, Henry James, and Joyce Cary.

Just about fifty years after the publication of *Tom Jones,* Jane Austen, refining the art, would write of the novel form as one in which potentially "the greatest powers of the mind are displayed, in which the most thorough knowledge of human nature, the happiest delineations of its varieties, the liveliest effusions of wit and humor are conveyed to the world in the best chosen language."[4] A hundred years later still, looking back over his own long career in the form and pressing his acute intelligence and sensibility to a considered judgment, Henry James would write that "the Novel remains still, under the right persuasion, the most independent, most elastic, most prodigious of literary forms."[5] Only the other day, too, Joyce Cary, in what turned out to be among his final words, spoke of the novel as a purveyor of truth, able to create and give meaning to human action, and always "concerned from first to last with morality."[6] But in 1749 Fielding's observations were not a summing up. They were in the nature of courageous innovation, a surveying of generally untraveled territory, a staking out of critical claims, and a pioneer's admission of responsibility in what he felt was "one of the most useful as well as entertaining of all Kinds of Writing."

QUALIFICATIONS FOR A NOVELIST

Four qualifications for a novelist are set out, exemplified, and defined in uncharacteristically plain fashion (IX, i), reappearing in the form of mock grandiloquent apostrophes invoking the assistance of Genius, Humanity, Learning, and Experience (XIII, i). Two of these, Learning and Experience, are treated again at the beginning of Book XIV..

(1) *Genius. Powers of Invention and Judgment.* The novelist, to be great, must possess powers of mind capable of quick and

---

[4] Jane Austen, *Northanger Abbey, Novels,* ed. R. W. Chapman, 3rd ed. (Oxford, 1948), V, 38.

[5] Henry James, Preface to *The Ambassadors,* in *The Art of the Novel,* ed. R. P. Blackmur (New York, 1934), p. 326.

[6] Joyce Cary, *Art and Reality* (Cambridge, England, 1958). "That is to say, the novelist addresses his meaning finally to the moral judgment. His whole apparatus of characters, plot, and description is designed to give knowledge of a world, his world, in which men, as he understands them, work out their destiny as moral beings " (p. 150).

sagacious penetration "into all Things within our Reach and
Knowledge, and of distinguishing their essential Differences"
(IX, i). His genius must assist his readers "to know Mankind
better than they know themselves" (XIII, i).

(2) *Humanity. Genuine Feeling.* The novelist will achieve his
effects not only by plotting and calculations but by rendering
shared emotions, those of tears as well as of laughter—"all those
strong Energies of a good Mind." This feeling for humanity is a
"constant Attendant on true Genius" (XIII, i).

(3) *Learning. Art. Rules.* "A competent Knowledge of History
and of the *Belles Lettres*" is essential in the novelist's equipment.
This knowledge is, however, to be considered as assistance to
purity and correctness, *not* as "Fetters on the natural Spriteliness
and Activity of the Imagination" (IX, i; XIV, i).

(4) *Experience.* First-hand observation is the only true source
for knowledge of human nature and manners, without which the
characters will be rendered with "neither the Justness nor Spirit
of an Original" (IX, i). Variety in fiction depends upon the
author's familiarity with high and low life; he must range "from
the Minister at his Levee, to the Bailiff in his Spunging-House;
from the Dutchess at her Drum, to the Landlady behind her
Bar" (XIII, i).

The eighteen prefaces deal with techniques and craftsmanship
in various moods of seriousness, sometimes at length, but often
in a passed-off phrase or two. My major headings below, some
of them in Fielding's own words, are set down here for the sake
of synthesis and organization; the emphasis, as faithful as I can
make it, is his.

2. THE CRAFT OF FICTION

(1) *The Highest Subject. Character above Action.* Human
nature with its true inconsistencies and variations, so difficult to
assess and render, is "the highest Subject (unless on very extra-

ordinary Occasions indeed) which presents itself." When a novelist is committed to the delineation of characters, individually and in their relationships, it is his business as an artist to "search into the most retired Recesses" of human nature and limit himself to what he honestly finds there. Such a limitation does *not* mean that "his Characters, or his Incidents, should be trite, common, or vulgar" (I, i; VIII, i). Challenging the attention of both the novelist and his reader, the act of probing into human nature calls for "some of the most excellent Faculties of the Mind" and for "greater Penetration" than that devoted to action alone : "it is a more useful Capacity to be able to foretel the Actions of Men in any Circumstance from their Characters; than to judge of their Characters from their Actions" (III, i).

(2) *"Conversation" of Character. Distinctions among Characters.* The first [printed as "Conservation" in the early editions of *Tom Jones*] is a term borrowed from dramatic criticism, Fielding says.[7] It denotes the knowledgeable suiting of actions to the unique nature of each individual character, so that what may seem "only wonderful and surprizing in one Man, may become improbable, or indeed impossible, when related of another" (VIII, i). By sustaining this precise sense of individuality within groups of similar persons who may be joined, for instance, by likeness in a profession or occupation, the novelist shows his skill. He may also show it by marking "the nice Distinction between two Persons actuated by the same Vice or Folly" (X, i).

(3) *Art of Imperfection.* The careful novelist will speckle his admirable characters with some "little Blemishes," which will "raise our Compassion rather than our Abhorrence," will introduce a glaring element of surprise, and will more likely arouse contemplation in the reader than would the expected wickedness of characters who are in no way admirable (X, i). As a lawyer and magistrate Fielding was pledged to the moral assumption

---

[7] See *OED*, "Conversation," No. 6: "Manner of conducting oneself in the world or in society; behaviour, mode or course of life."

that every charge must be assessed individually and dispassion-
ately; as a novelist he was pledged to the view that human nature
is inescapably checkered, and that he could therefore "censure
the Action, without conceiving any absolute Detestation of the
Person" (VII, i).

(4) *Mental Entertainment. The Novelist's Job of Skill*. Because
the single subject of human nature prevails in most fiction, good
or bad, "the Excellence of the mental Entertainment consists less
in the Subject, than in the Author's Skill in well dressing it up."
Such a dressing, Fielding says, is to be seen in the structural
contrast of country and city manners in *Tom Jones* (I, i). When
he frequently admonishes his readers to wake up and pay attention to his artful arrangement of materials — less outrageously
though than the readers of *Tristram Shandy* were later to be
prodded and admonished — Fielding is asserting the novelist's job
as one of skill.

(5) *Time and the Dramatic Scene*. Fielding had published
twenty-two dramatic pieces, not counting dramatic collaborations,
revisions, and translations, and must have been as conscious as
any man could be, of how playwrights manipulate the time
element to hold characters convincingly in sustained action on
the stage. In the novel as well as on the stage, his technique is
that of focusing upon dramatic scenes. Because only the extraordinary scenes will be opened "at large to our Reader," some
chapters will be longer than others; there will be "some that
contain only the Time of a single Day, and others that comprise
Years" (II, i; III, i).

(6) *Variety and Ornamental Parts. The Device of Amusement*.
Through variety and contrast the novelist may establish mood,
change pace, relieve tension, maintain interest, "prepare the Mind
of the Reader," and "refresh the Mind" (IV, i). One function of
the critical prefaces, Fielding says, is that of contrast: they are
"so many Scenes of *Serious* [matter] artfully interwoven" (V, i).
Toward the close of *Tom Jones* he confides to his reader that his

endeavors to be amusing are one means of holding interest in his subject, saying that if he has "indulged any pleasantry" for entertainment's sake, it was to "prevent thee from taking a Nap" (XVIII, i).

(7) *The Marvelous. Surprise.* In general the novelist should respect the observable limits of human nature : no supernatural aid can deliver the hero of a novel from his torments (VIII, i; XVII, i). But the truly marvelous — not the supernatural or incredible — may very well show itself if the novelist severely confines himself to what might really happen. He must transcribe matters of human nature "as he finds them," even though they are amazing, extraordinary, or outlandish; and "if he thus keep within the Rules of Credibility, the more he can surprise the Reader, the more he will engage his Attention, and the more he will charm him" (VIII, i).

Because it is customary to remark that novelists nowadays are less certain of their amorphous, mass reading public than were eighteenth-century novelists, who comfortably knew the backgrounds and tastes of their fixed number of readers, it is usually assumed that Fielding and his contemporaries could gauge their art with relative ease. But to know your audience is to know its unpreparedness, its insensitivity, its hard-skinned prejudicial attitudes, its dismal responses to all the stock clues, its lack of appreciation, and its infusion of simple mouth-breathing stupidity. Yet the novelist may not treat his readers like the misanthrope who had the theater ceiling open wide to rain ordure upon the audience. Unless he is writing merely for himself the novelist must love his reader and attempt to teach him through entertainment. He must guide his reader through fiction's feigning world.

Although he was perfectly aware that many readers, like Samuel Richardson, would withhold their full attention and sympathy, Fielding tried to consider his audience genially as friends and companions on a journey. Little could be done about the Richardsons; but some of the audience could be trained to appreciate the comic novel as a form of art that requires the reader's full participation. A novel worthy of close reading, Fielding wrote in the Preface to his sister Sarah's *David Simple* (1744), "*consists in a vast Penetration into human Nature, a deep and profound Discernment of all the Mazes, Windings, and Labyrinths, which perplex the Heart of man to such a degree, that he is himself often incapable of seeing through them; and as this is the greatest, noblest, and rarest of all the Talents which constitute a Genius; so a much larger Share of this Talent is necessary, even to recognize these Discoveries, when they are laid before us, than fall to the share of a common Reader.*" The trained, uncommon reader, he says in several of the prefatory chapters in *Tom Jones*, must lend his closest attention to the art of reading.

3. THE ART OF READING FICTION

(1) *Prejudicial Responses.* The example of Black George's not returning the £500 to Tom is used to illustrate how groups of readers would react differently to a single incident : some with "scurrilous Reproach"; some by expecting Black George's punishment; some by outraged objections to villainy unpunished; some by calling it evil but lifelike; some by terming it "low"; and some by suspending all responses until the "proper" attitude is certain. But the author, who has a rather different intention in mind, believes that "the man of Candour and of true Understanding, is never hasty to condemn" (VII, i). In the reading of a novel, such sensibility would not only be moral but artistic as well; for the reader must creatively assist the author and trust his judgments as they are finally revealed.

(2) *The Significant Entirety.* The reader must learn to submit to the grand pattern of the work in its significant entirety. He must not object too quickly to seeming violations of "our main

Design," pointing a finger at what he considers a "Fault with any of its Parts, without knowing the Manner in which the Whole is connected" (X, i). The novel must be seen and judged as a whole, not objected to because of a displeasing incident or chapter. In any extended, variegated work someone's taste is certain to be offended (XI, i).

(3) *Sympathetic Involvement.* In making moral judgments the reader must exercise his powers of sympathy and imagination, not judging only by his own experience but imagining himself in other people's shoes. "Why will we not modestly observe the same Rule in judging of the Good, as well as the Evil of others? Or why in any Case, will we, as *Shakespear* phrases it, 'put the World in our own Person'?" (VI, i). The reader must not be hasty to condemn a characterization upon learning that it is not perfect (X, i). The creative art of reading requires sufficient "Historic or Poetic Faith" to believe what has not been personally experienced. Again, the reader must entrust himself in the author's hands (VIII, i). If, as a reader, you do not bring sympathy and imagination to moral judgments, "you have, I assure you, already read more than you have understood; and it would be wiser to pursue your Business, or your Pleasures (such as they are) than to throw away any more of your Time in reading what you can neither taste nor comprehend" (VI, i).

(4) *Generalizations from Individuals.* Persons in novels are not properly to be considered "characters" as the word was used in seventeenth-century "characters" of "the Hen-Pecked Husband," "The Generall Artist," "The Scholar," etc., intended to represent types. The novel-reader is not to conclude general conduct from representations of individual characters. Lady Bellaston, for example, who keeps Tom as her paid lover and urges Lord Fellamar to rape Sophia, does not necessarily reflect the "general Conduct of Women of fashion"; nor is one to assume that "every Clergyman was represented by *Thwackum,* or every Soldier by Ensign *Northerton*" (XIV, i).

The prefatory chapters have real interest in their own right, although William Empson has recently chosen to refer to them as "literary prattle."[8] They have never, so far as I know, been printed together separate from the novel, although W. Somerset Maugham has edited *Tom Jones* omitting the prefaces. The fullest function of the prefaces is in connection with the books of *Tom Jones* that follow them. Fielding pretends that most of them "may as properly be prefixed to any other Book in this History as to that which they introduce" (XII, i); but that is not quite true.

Persons who have "greatly admired" Fielding's prefaces, Maugham says, must have done so "because they were not interested in the novel as a novel."[9] On the contrary, besides laying out the future of the novel form with shrewd insight, the prefaces are demonstrably working parts of the machinery of *Tom Jones*. Fielding's "literary" essays contribute artfully to the novel's illusion of "life."[10]

---

[8] William Empson, "Tom Jones," *Kenyon Review*, XX (Spring, 1958), 233.

[9] W. Somerset Maugham, *Great Novelists and Their Novels* (Philadelphia and Toronto, 1948), p. 74.

[10] The matter introductory to Books I and II serves as general preparation for the reading of the novel; and the first chapter of Book XVIII assists in winding up the business of all the preceding pages. Book III, i, distinguishing between inner and outer manifestations of character, gives clues to what will later be revealed about some of the characters, especially Bridget, Tom's real mother. Book IV, i, turning lyrical, announces that the author is "about to introduce the Heroine," Sophia; and Book V, i, stating that "the finest Brilliant requires a Foil," prepares for the choice Tom must make between Sophia and Molly Seagrim. Book VI, i, entitled "Of Love," does indeed dwell on that subject as do the chapters that follow.

Similar connections appear in most of the prefatory chapters. The introductions to Books IX and X, restating the qualifications for a responsible novelist and warning the reader against acting "too hastily to condemn" a character, lead into Tom's crucial seduction by Mrs. Waters. Book XIV, i, discussing "Upper Life," prepares for a contrasting of the dissipations of Lady Bellaston with the decencies of little Nancy Miller. The discrepancy between virtue and happiness, dealt with in XV, i, is dramatized in the chapters that follow in that book. And a discussion of ancient and modern ways of "delivering a Hero" in XVII, i, leads into Tom's deliverance from all the charges against him.

VI

The Foundling and the Prince
Tom Jones

Ham. Alas poore Ghost.
Gho. Pitty me not, but lend thy serious hearing
To what I shall unfold.
Ham. Speake, I am bound to heare.

Tom Jones bears a relationship to the English novel similar to
that of *Hamlet* to the drama, and its perfections and imper-
fections, like those of *Hamlet,* have long been a subject for controversy. "Is there truth, or only a vast exaggeration, in the almost
unanimous verdict of modern critics respecting the supreme
excellence of *Tom Jones* as a work of art? We say, as a work of
art, because that is the only ground for serious discussion." So
wrote George Henry Lewes (leaving his name unsigned) in *Blackwood's Edinburgh Magazine* just a hundred years ago, in March,
1860. As a supreme work of art rather than as the biographical
document, latitudinarian tract, or inflammatory joke book that
some commentators have imagined it to be, *Tom Jones* had earlier
been singled out by Coleridge, who had exclaimed over its plot:
a perfect one, like the plots of *Oedipus Tyrannus* and *The
Alchemist.* Thackeray, who endeavored to imitate the plot in his
own fiction, also exclaimed that it was nearly perfect.

Perfect in what way? George Henry Lewes went on to inquire.
It was clear to him that Thackeray's judgment was woefully
mistaken, and that, if the object of construction in a novel is "to

free the story from all superfluity . . . in incident, dialogue, description, or character," then "*Tom Jones,* so far from being a masterpiece of construction is, in truth, a very ill-constructed novel." For contrast Lewes remarked on the exquisite organic unity of *Pride and Prejudice.* Most of *Tom Jones* seemed to him merely episodic : after Book VI, a third of the way through the work, when Tom has fallen from grace and has been turned out of Squire Allworthy's Paradise Hall, Fielding relaxes his grasp on his constructive art and produces merely a succession of episodes — "simply because he wanted to produce the effect of variety, and was not artist enough to make the variety spring from and tend to unity." To conclude his depreciatory remarks Lewes dismissed the construction of *Tom Jones* as "essentially bad of its kind, and the kind very low; so far from there being any consummate art, such as delicate instinct or steady reflection would have suggested, there is only the vulgar artifice of the ordinary novelist, rendered more effective than usual by an unusual audacity and animation."[1]

Thackeray, in an attempt to defend Fielding's art and his own against this onslaught, offered praise for "the brave old master," but his defense was too postured and exclamatory to have done much good : "Why, did not a wiseacre in *Blackwood's Magazine* lately fall foul of *Tom Jones?* O hypercritic !" He had no reply for *Tom Jones* as a work of art ("the only ground for serious discussion"). Evidently Thackeray was unaware that the attacker was Lewes, and he could hardly have known that Lewes, who said he hoped his essay would be a "stunner," had used even stronger language in his original manuscript, to which John Blackwood, as editor, had objected : "coarse drollery," for instance, as the chief merit of *Tom Jones,* and "shallow circumscribed nature" to characterize Fielding himself. Thackeray did

---

[1] George Henry Lewes, " A Word about Tom Jones," *Blackwood's Edinburgh Magazine,* LXXXVII (March, 1860), 331–341.

nothing to restore the epithet of "perfect" to the plot.[2]

Some twentieth-century commentators have painstakingly outlined the chronology of events in *Tom Jones,* setting Part Two (Books VII–XII, on the road from Paradise Hall to London) at the end of November, 1745, and Part Three (Books XIII–XVIII, in London) during December of that year, occasionally dating episodes down to the hour.[3] In "A Study of the Structure of *Tom Jones*" one commentator has attempted to demonstrate at length that the shape of the novel is controlled by the idea of latitudinarian benevolism enforced by a social vision that imposes a beneficent design over all hateful and disintegrating impulses. In "Structural Techniques in *Tom Jones*" another commentator has ingeniously categorized and cited examples of "plot division," "spatial and temporal verisimilitude," "parallelism," "the planned reappearance," "the undisclosed motive," "the blurred consequence," "the minute cause," and "the alternative interpretation," showing for example how even the interpolated "Man of the Hill" interlude fits into place under certain of these headings. So much for the studies which try to explain elements that make the plot perfect.[4]

In his long essay on "The Plot of *Tom Jones,*" R. S. Crane argues for recognition of interfunctioning elements in the novel and invites appreciation for its dynamic "system of actions," to which "plot," however perfect, is only contributory. Although it was certainly not Mr. Crane's intention to diminish the reputation of *Tom Jones* for our time, he does somewhat diminish it by

[2] William Makepeace Thackeray, *The Cornhill Magazine,* II (July, 1860), 124; George Henry Lewes to John Blackwood [16 January, 1860], and John Blackwood to Lewes, 23 January, 1860, in *The George Eliot Letters,* ed. Gordon S. Haight (New Haven, 1954), III, 249, 251.

[3] See Frederick S. Dickson, "The Chronology of *Tom Jones,*" *The Library,* 3 series VIII (July, 1917), 218–224, and F. Homes Dudden, *Henry Fielding: His Life, Works, and Times* (Oxford, 1952), II, 597–615.

[4] Robert Chidester Meredith, "Henry Fielding and the Idea of Benevolence: A Study of the Structure of *Tom Jones,*" unpubl. diss. Univ. of Wisconsin (1955); James J. Lynch, "Structural Techniques in *Tom Jones,*" *Zeitschrift für Anglistik und Amerikanistik,* VII (1959), 5–16.

concluding, after a lengthy summary of the story, that in it Fielding relies mostly "on techniques or narrative now largely abandoned by novelists who have learned their art since the middle of the nineteenth century." Specifically, Mr. Crane says that *Tom Jones* reaches its audience through an elaborately contrived "statement" of external action rather than through a "rendering" of its matter. A. A. Parker, unsympathetically comparing *Tom Jones* with *Don Quixote,* describes how Fielding's achievement is limited by his mere episodic regularity, "outward form regulated by fixed precepts," a "superficial quality of formal neatness," and "external symmetry and polish" — inferior to Cervantes's deeper rendering of the inner significance of characters who develop progressively. And E. M. W. Tillyard writes that (like Lewes) he is not much impressed by the so-called "perfect way *Tom Jones* is plotted. There is too much plot, too many surprising turns. These end by wearying . . . ."[5]

"Perfect for what?" Ian Watt echoes in reference to the plot. "Not, certainly, for the exploration of character and of personal relations . . . . Fielding does not make any attempt to individualise his characters." Unlike Lewes and Tillyard, who objected to a surfeit of episodes in the plot, Mr. Watt admires the "remarkably fine control in it" but thinks it *too* neat and strong in its effects, at the expense of characterization. When a novel all finally fits into place, like a complicated jig-saw puzzle or a well-made detective story, leaving no loose pieces, it is likely to arouse suspicion or resentment in modern critics who would concur with E. M. Forster that a novel with a truly "fine" plot will leave a sense, not of clues and jig-saw pieces, but "of something aesthetically compact" and finally beautiful in its unfolding.[6]

    [5] R. S. Crane, " The Concept of Plot and the Plot of *Tom Jones," Critics and Criticism* (abridged), ed. R. S. Crane (Chicago, 1957), pp. 62–93; A. A. Parker, " Fielding and the Structure of *Don Quixote," Bulletin of Hispanic Studies,* XXXIII (January, 1956), 1–16; E. M. W. Tillyard, *The Epic Strain in the English Novel* (London, 1958), pp. 51–58.
    [6] Ian Watt, *The Rise of the Novel* (Berkeley and Los Angeles, 1957), pp. 269, 272; E. M. Forster, *Aspects of the Novel* (New York, 1927), p. 133.

George Henry Lewes has largely had his way in creating doubts about the "supreme excellence of *Tom Jones* as a work of art." Not that any critic of reputation has ever denied that *Tom Jones* is other than marvelous as a reading experience; but critics have been puzzled to explain the marvel. Henry James, who was dreadfully puzzled, finally decided that, besides Tom's health and vigor amounting "almost to his having a mind," Fielding's own mind, humor, and style "somehow really enlarge, make every one and every thing important." James's revealing word, which demolishes faith in fictional "techniques," is his "somehow."[7]

Tom Jones undeservedly holds its fame, one American critic explains, because it is "the most mechanically plotted of English novels from initial intrigue to final marriage," its events can be intricately diagrammed, and because a conversation early in the novel will certainly have consequences later on, thus satisfying "Industrial Man," for whom "construction," "form," and "blueprint" are indistinguishable.[8] Still another American critic, also concerned with "Industrial Man" and himself the author of novels, writes that Fielding's idea of a plot was simply to leave no gaps unfilled : "Fielding was one of the most insidious influences ever functioning on English letters," and *Tom Jones* owes its lingering renown to the depraved taste of persons who value matter above spirit, prefer trash to literature, and "do not know either to read or think." And further from the same critic :

A casual comparison of the morality of *Tom Jones* and the morality of *Hamlet* will show the place Fielding should hold in English literature. In *Tom Jones* the hero believes momentarily that he has committed incest, but when he learns that mechanically he did not, his worry is dropped, which is to indicate that the whole problem of morals to Fielding is one of outer circumstance and not spirit. He is, in fact, a thorough materialist masquerading as a

---

[7] Henry James, Preface to *The Princess Casamassima*, in *The Art of the Novel*, ed. R. P. Blackmur (New York, 1934), p. 68.

[8] Hugh Kenner, *Wyndham Lewis* (Norfolk, Conn., 1954), pp. 9–10, and *The Poetry of Ezra Pound* (Norfolk, Conn., n. d.), p. 55.

moralist. In *Hamlet* the Prince is driven mad, not by the technical accomplishment of incest but by the idea of it . . . . The difference between Fielding and Shakespeare in this is the same as the difference between *How to Win Friends and Influence People* and the Sermon on the Mount, namely a difference in attitude : huckstering and religion.*

The challenge is too tempting to ignore; or, more truthfully, the idea of comparing Tom Jones and Hamlet, the Foundling and the Prince, is too outrageous to pass by. More suitably perhaps, Tom should be joined for comparison with Charles Surface, who may be descended from him : both are mildly rakish, both have hearts of gold, and both suffer in the shadow of black-hearted, hypocritical brothers. But by looking at Tom alongside Hamlet I may be able to arrive at a useful remark or two about (1) Fielding's art of characterization, (2) the "inner," "concealed," or "poetic" functioning of episodes which unify his plot, and (3) the nature of comic fiction.

Near the end of *Tom Jones* (XVI, v) Fielding has placed an episode usually thought of as one of his set-pieces which may be read with pleasure outside the context of the novel as a whole. As such in anthologies and in *The Beauties of Fielding* the episode might bear the title "Jones and Partridge at the Theatre." Fielding's own chapter-heading reads "In Which Jones receives a letter from Sophia, and goes to a play with Mrs. Miller and Partridge." Mrs. Miller's younger daughter is with them when they take their places in the first row of the first gallery.

Before the performance of the play begins, Partridge expresses his wonder at the musicians and at the prodigal burning of candles for illumination. Then, closely watching the play, he inquires about the identity of a figure in armor but cannot at first be persuaded that it is a ghost : "No, no Sir, Ghosts don't appear in such Dresses as that, neither." Convinced, however, by Hamlet's

---

* Robert O. Bowen, "Modern Gothic Prose," *New Ventures*, I (1954), 54–61.

scene with the ghost, he defends his own trembling and argues
that "if that little Man there upon the Stage is not frightened, I
never saw any Man frightened in my Life." He offers another
tribute to Garrick's realistic acting during the scene in Gertrude's
apartment when the ghost again appears: "There, Sir, now;
what say you now? Is he frightened now or no?" And he justifies
Hamlet's berating and shaking his mother, vowing that "If she
was my own Mother, I should serve her so." During the play
within the play, Partridge blesses himself that he has never been
guilty of murder. He is critical of the grave-digging scene. Then,
at the end of the play, when Tom inquires which of the actors
he liked best, Partridge names the king. "'Indeed, Mr. *Partridge*,'
says Mrs. *Miller*, 'you are not of the same Opinion with the
Town; for they are all agreed, that *Hamlet* is acted by the best
player who was ever on the Stage.'"

" He the best Player !" cries *Partridge* with a contemptuous Sneer,
" why, I could act as well as he myself. I am sure if I had seen a
Ghost, I should have looked in the very same Manner, and done
just as he did. And then, to be sure, in that Scene, as you call it,
between him and his Mother, where you told me he acted so fine,
why, Lord help me, any Man, that is, any good Man, that had such
a Mother, would have done exactly the same. I know you are only
joking with me; but, indeed, Madam, though I was never at a Play
in *London*, yet I have seen Acting before in the Country; and the
King for my Money; he speaks all his Words distinctly, half as loud
again as the other. — Anybody may see he is an Actor."

This is a model of humorous characterization. Partridge's agree-
able natural innocence is delightful. He cannot avoid speaking
and acting in a manner that distinguishes him oddly from the
people around him in the theater. Tom Jones, too, is individ-
ualized in this scene — naturally superior, "in the know," and
benignly amused at the comments of his companion. "Why
Partridge, you exceed my Expectations. You enjoy the Play more
than I conceived possible," Tom rather loftily remarks. In the

short time of their residence in London, Tom has seemingly become a part of the sophisticated metropolis, whereas Partridge has lost none of his country manners and ingenuousness. Indeed, it was Partridge more than Garrick that Tom looked to for his diversion in the theater : "For as *Jones* had really that Taste for Humour which many affect, he expected to enjoy much Entertainment in the Criticisms of *Partridge;* from whom he expected the simple Dictates of Nature, unimproved indeed, but likewise unadulterated by Art." The reader genuinely shares Tom's amusement at Partridge's comments; but the reader also senses a coolness in Fielding's presentation of Tom here. In *Joseph Andrews,* as a clue to Joseph's true nobility of spirit, Fielding had him quote with feeling from *Macbeth;* and Tom would do well to share some of Partridge's ingenuous country reaction to the ghost of Hamlet's father.

For while Tom sits in the theater, forces are moving in upon him to make him share Hamlet's experiences : swordplay, "murder," his mother's "incest," the return of his father's "ghost," accusations, and attempts upon his life. Just as Partridge has missed the point of the performance by applauding the king ("While the truest and finest Strokes of Nature, represented by a judicious and just Actor, pass unobserved and disregarded"[10]), Tom has lacked the insight to recognize that the play is about himself. Before he leaves the theater Mrs. Fitzpatrick comes to him and makes an appointment for the next day, leading to the "tragical Incident" in which Tom seems to have killed Mr. Fitzpatrick; Lord Fellamar's men then place Tom in the hands of a civil magistrate (XVI, ix–x). Squire Allworthy, convinced by Blifil of Tom's complete infamy, arrives in London to assist Blifil's wooing of Sophia on "that Evening when Mr. *Jones,* as we have seen, was diverting himself with *Partridge* at the Play" (XVI, vi). Lady Bellaston makes known Tom's letter proposing marriage to

    [10] Henry Fielding, "Essay on the Knowledge of the Characters of Men," *Miscellanies* (1743).

her, thus appearing to end any possibility of his ever reconciling Sophia to him. "I am indifferent as to what happens to me," Tom says: "for tho' I am convinced I am not guilty of Murder in the Eye of the Law, yet the Weight of Blood I find intolerable upon my Mind" (XVI, x).

And while he is a prisoner at the Gatehouse, awaiting possible death by hanging, Tom is told that it was his own mother with whom he lay in the inn at Upton (XVIII, ii). He falls into agonies of despair and is "almost raving mad." "Sure, Fortune will never have done with me 'till she hath driven me to Distraction. But why do I blame Fortune? I am myself the Cause of all my Misery. All the dreadful Mischiefs which have befallen me, are the Consequences only of my own Folly and Vice . . . . O good Heaven! Incest—with a Mother! To what am I reserved!" The young man who went to a performance of *Hamlet* in order to be amused by "the simple Dictates of Nature, unimproved," has himself become Hamlet.

Hamlet and Tom Jones are both unheroic heroes who act impulsively, arouse disapproval, accuse themselves, and are involved in violence although they are deterred from further violence by moral scruples, prudence, or Christian ethics. Both Hamlet and Tom have some badness in their natures, both are passionate individualists, both are caught in a series of events half mockery and half horror, and both are haunted by their fathers' spirits.

But unlike the tragic hero who, at the moment of his deepest humiliation, despair, or death, is allowed flashing glimpses of human meaningfulness and of possible regeneration, Tom Jones, inhabiting an ultimately comic world, is snatched away from his distresses no matter how hopeless: all losses are restored, and gifts hasten to him. The conclusion is not merely one of vision but of legacy. Tom almost at once learns that he is guilty of neither incest nor murder, is reconciled with his patron, receives Sophia in marriage, and assumes his true identity, not as " Tom

Jones " but as Allworthy's heir and the son of Summer (we are told that "the Sun never shone upon" a finer man than Mr. Summer, Tom's father, no longer ghost-like and mysterious). Tom is a Hamlet who learns that he has not killed Polonius, learns that he has been mistaken about his mother, happily marries his Ophelia, forgives the villain but banishes him, rewards his faithful Horatio, and returns to his native land to create a little kingdom for himself. It is the difference between tragedy and comedy.

Comedy is distinguished by "the avoidance of the terrible outcome of the events which were threatened in tragedy."[11] When the hero in comedy, accused of unspeakable crimes, is rolled down the rocks and pushed into the lion's den, he discovers of course that the lion is the king in disguise and that his painful trials have been tests of his worthiness to marry the princess. When Tom thinks he is guilty of incest, the Wheel of Fortune can turn him no lower and his fortunes must rise if the novel remains true to its comic nature. The possibility of incest, Northrop Frye points out, forms "one of the minor themes of comedy." And Frye notes that "Tom Jones in the final book, accused of murder, incest, debt, and double-dealing, cast off by friends, guardian, and sweetheart, is a woeful figure indeed before all these turn into illusions."[12]

According to José Ortega y Gasset the novel form is characterized by a "comic sting." The tragic is differentiated from the comic, he says, in the same way that "wishing to be" differs from "believing that one already is." "The transference on a heroic scale from the plane of will to that of perception causes the involution of tragedy, its disintegration—and makes comedy of it. The mirage is seen as nothing but mirage."[13] In tragedy,

---

[11] James Feibleman, *In Praise of Comedy* (New York, 1939), p. 77. Here Feibleman is summarizing Plato's theory of the comic.

[12] Northrop Frye, *Anatomy of Criticism* (Princeton, 1957), pp. 178–179, 181.

[13] José Ortega y Gasset, "The Nature of the Novel," trans. Evelyn Rugg and Diego Marín, *The Hudson Review*, X (Spring, 1957), 32, 39.

murder and incest are portentous and crushing; but the point
of comedy is that murder and incest prove only "technical":
they are mirages that the sunlight dispels. The sunlight of comedy
accompanies a reversal of situation and fortunes (the *peripeteia*),
a discovery such as that of the identity of persons, and a recovery
of friendships. In tragedy the hero may be driven mad by remorse
or hatred, but in comedy "the deadliest of legendary foes, like
Orestes and Aegisthus, become friends, and quit the stage without
any one slaying or being slain."[14] The feigning of comedy seems
sometimes to proceed one step beyond or away from the feigning
of tragedy; for comedy often presents and follows tragic matter
into the maw of disaster, before the reversal. Such comedy is
doubly feigned.

Before introducing the discoveries and reversals of the plot to
the reader, Fielding pauses to comment on the difference between
tragic and comic writing. The work of a tragic writer is completed,
he says, when the principal characters are brought "to the highest
pitch of human Misery" and "a Murder or two and a few moral
Sentences" are added for good measure. But the work of a comic
writer is done when he manages to lift the favorite characters
"out of their present Anguish and to land them at last on the
Shore of Happiness." This, he says not entirely in jest, seems to
him "a much harder Task" than that of the writer of tragedy
(XVII, i).

If George Henry Lewes and some later critics had been willing
to read *Tom Jones* in the light of Fielding's own comments on
the nature of comic fiction, and if they had not prejudicially
dubbed his great talent, in Lewes's phrase, as "only the vulgar
artifice of the ordinary novelist," they might have gained more
appreciation for his complexity, depth, and ability to render

---

[14] Lane Cooper, *An Aristotelian Theory of Comedy* (New York, 1922),
p. 201. Cooper writes: "If we admit the reality of a comic catharsis, we
must grant that the effect proceeds from the use, in comedy, of dramatic
suspense, and from the arousal and defeat of our expectations in various
ways" (p. 68).

inner significances beneath a bright, amusing surface. The artifice through which Fielding beautifully unfolds character, story, and theme, in the Hamlet scene, is of a very high order. It is artifice which amusingly entertains, ingeniously performs constructive duties important to the meaningful entirety of the novel, and invites the reader to a reconsideration of moral evaluations. If the reader has been sympathetically but unwarily involved with Tom at the play, and has shared Tom's supercilious attitude towards Partridge's simple confusion of real and stage worlds, the reader should also, vicariously, share Tom's punishment. The reader joins Tom, for a while, in the role of a comic Hamlet.[15]

---

[15] Wilbur L. Cross drew a likeness between Prince and Foundling by saying that " As in ' Hamlet,' the problem of ' Tom Jones ' is the hero himself. Not because Fielding is obscure, but because the character raises certain moral questions, humorously casuistical, on which men are bound to differ."—*The History of Henry Fielding* (New Haven, 1918), II, 212. In " Jungian " terms Hamlet and Tom are alike in their quest for a father. Lacking paternal authority they are both somewhat immature or undisciplined, both unwilling or unable to assume a responsible place in the society of men. As unheroic heroes both Hamlet and Tom are engaged in " separation," " initiation," and " return " in their mythological rites of passage described by Jung. Tom passes through a series of tests during his journey without permanent damage to his person or character. In the last three chapters of the novel, after the comic reversals and discoveries, he assumes the role of father by advising Allworthy concerning the proper dispensation for Blifil, Black George, and others. As Hamlet finally fulfills the ghost's commands and joins his father in death, Tom gains prudence, enters maturity, and is himself literally a father as the novel ends.

VII

Here the Book Dropt from Her Hand

Tom Jones

Euph. *We are willing to join with you in paying the tribute due to Fielding's Genius, humour, and knowledge of mankind, but he certainly painted human nature as* it is, ra[ther] *than as* it ought to be. — *Clara Reeve.*[1]

Although Tom Jones has sometimes been called Fielding's sentimental argument for "goodness," alien to the comic mode of the novel that bears his name, he receives his share of ridicule, as we have seen in the *Hamlet* episode.[2] But Sophia Western, in whom Tom's virtue of good nature is complemented by chastity and admirable prudence, is less palpably comic. In her, all virtues and feminine beauties seem to be graciously combined. She is the attractive, good, redeeming woman who finally makes her man complete. Even she, however, is portrayed within the scope of Fielding's comic sensibility, and her character is shaped for the reader by means of ironical commentary.

For Sophia's introduction into the story, Fielding sets a rhetorically elaborate stage, strewing flowers, as the custom is, he says, before the entrance of great personages at a coronation: "Our Intention, in short, is to introduce our Heroine with the utmost

---

[1] Euphrasia, in *The Progress of Romance,* 1785, Facsimile Text Society (New York, 1930), p. 141.

[2] For defense of Tom as a comic character, see E. N. Hooker, " Humour in the Age of Pope," *Huntington Library Quarterly,* IV (August, 1948), 382–383.

Solemnity in our Power, with an Elevation of Stile, and all other Circumstances proper to raise the Veneration of our Reader" (IV, i). Beneath the heading "A SHORT HINT OF WHAT WE CAN DO IN THE SUBLIME, AND A DESCRIPTION OF MISS *SOPHIA WESTERN*," ˋFielding announces his heroine's first appearance :

Hushed be every ruder Breath. May the heathen Ruler of the Winds confine in iron Chains the boisterous Limbs of noisy *Boreas,* and the sharp-pointed Nose of bitter-biting *Eurus.* Do thee, sweet *Zephyrus,* rising from thy fragrant Bed, mount the western sky, and lead on those delicious Gales, the Charms of which call forth the lovely *Flora* from her Chamber, perfumed with pearly Dews, when on the first of *June,* her Birth-day, the blooming Maid, in loose Attire, gently trips it over the verdant Mead, where every Flower rises to do her Homage, 'till the whole Field becomes enamelled, and Colours contend with Sweets which shall ravish her most. (IV, ii)

That overture to Sophia's entrance may not "raise the Veneration" of the reader, but as an announced exercise in "sublime" language, it bookishly and in the spirit of poetry prepares the way for a heroine as fresh and beautiful as Spring. It is the kind of artificial apostrophe to be read not only in much of the bad poetry of Fielding's day, but in good poetry like the odes of Gray. It may also be read in Boswell's journal when, demurring at Johnson's scorn for "sublime ideas" of Nature, he proves to himself what *he* can do "in the sublime" by writing a passage in the mood of "O Arthur Seat, thou venerable mountain!"[3] For Fielding this rhetoric is a device for rejecting rhetoric, preparatory to the entrance of a heroine who, however lovely, is not a goddess but very much a human being. She cannot live up to the absurd, bookish sublimity of the introductory rhetoric, nor would the reader wish her to; after six paragraphs of introduction she steps

---

[3] James Boswell, 6 July, 1763, *Boswell's London Journal, 1762–1763,* ed. F. A. Pottle (New York, 1950), p. 294.

down from the flower-strewn stage: "*Sophia* then, the only Daughter of Mr. *Western,* was a middlesized Woman; but rather inclining to tall." Fielding's orchestration of pretentious and literal styles is one of his means for suggesting the mixed nature of life itself. He laughs neither at the "sublime" rhetoric nor at the flat statement of "fact" in his fiction; but he wants the reader to share his amusement at their gently mocking, glaring mixture.

The convincing power of fiction and the elusiveness of reality are amusingly contrasted in the scene described by Fielding as "the most tragical Matter in our whole History." It is the scene of Lord Fellamar's attempt to rape Sophia in Lady Bellaston's house. Attracted by Sophia's charms when he rescued her from a theater riot, Fellamar had called upon her; but he was of less interest to Sophia than to Lady Bellaston, for she saw in him a way to render the girl no longer a rival for Tom Jones's affections. Fellamar was reluctant to commit violence, but after Lady Bellaston had intimidated him, shamed him, and inflamed his passions, he agreed to the act. She thought that "the ravished *Sophia* would easily be brought to consent" to marriage, thus removing the girl "from being any further Obstruction to her Amour with *Jones.*" This was a variation on the central symbolic incident in Richardson's *Clarissa,* in which the heroine was to be offered marriage only after she had in fact been raped. Fielding begins:

The Clock had now struck Seven, and poor *Sophia,* alone and melancholy, sat reading a Tragedy. It was the *Fatal Marriage,* and she was now come to that Part where the poor, distrest *Isabella* disposes of her Wedding-Ring.

Here the Book dropt from her Hand, and a Shower of Tears ran down into her Bosom. (XV, v)

The striking of the clock lets us know, as Sophia does not know, what is in store for her, for we have earlier been told that "The next Evening at Seven was appointed for the fatal Purpose . . ." (XV, iii). Then we have been told that the narrative will "hasten to the fatal Hour, when every Thing was prepared for the Destruction of poor *Sophia*" (XV, iv). Repetition of the word "fatal" leads to the name of the tragedy that appeals to Sophia's lachrymose sensibilities in this scene : Thomas Southerne's *The Fatal Marriage; or, The Innocent Adultery* (1694), a sentimental or "pathetic" tragedy in blank verse. In Southerne's play, as in Hill's *The Fatal Extravagance* (1721), Hewitt's *The Fatal Falsehood* (1733), and Lillo's *The Fatal Curiosity* (1736, with a Prologue by Fielding), "fatal" denotes ruinous episodes culminating in death. That is also the "literary" meaning of the word in this scene in *Tom Jones,* although its meaning in the action here is merely that of "prearranged" and perhaps "distressing."

In *The Fatal Marriage* Isabella has left a nunnery to marry Biron. Marrying against his father's wishes, Biron is disinherited in favor of his scheming brother Carlos; and when Biron is reported killed at war, Isabella is left unprotected, is renounced, and is humiliated. Concealing his knowledge that Biron is still alive, Carlos encourages Isabella to marry Villeroy; after she does so, Biron returns. Carlos's villainy is unmasked, but not before he has mortally wounded Biron, and Isabella, the innocent adultress, has killed herself.[4] The scene in which Isabella " disposes of her Wedding-Ring" occurs in Act II, just before she receives the offer of marriage from Villeroy. Almost destitute, distracted, and attended only by her faithful nurse, she must sell her wedding ring, her last possession :

> *This Ring is all I've left of Value now:*
> *'Twas given me by my Husband: His first Gift*
> *Upon our Marriage: I have always kept it,*
> *With my best Care, the Treasure next my Life:*
> *And now but part with it, to support Life:*
> *Which only can be dearer. Take it Nurse . . . .*

---

[4] See J. W. Dodds, *Thomas Southerne, Dramatist* (New Haven, 1933), pp. 158–162; and R. G. Noyes, *The Neglected Muse: Restoration and Eighteenth-Century Tragedy in the Novel (1740–1780),* Brown University Studies, XXIV (Providence, R. I., 1958), 79.

> *Thinking will make me mad: Why must I think,*
> *When no Thought brings me Comfort? . . .*
> *Nurse.* . . . . what will you do, Madam?
> *Isa.*   Do! nothing, no, for I am born to suffer.

It is at this point in *The Fatal Marriage,* then, that "poor *Sophia*," usually poised and charmingly sensible, equates her own situation with that of "the poor, distrest *Isabella*," and begins to cry. Fielding suggests that, in her "melancholy" mood, she remembers how she is cut off from Tom and from her father; she remembers how she has been harried to accept unwelcome suitors, and she feels that she too is "born to suffer." Her sympathetic involvement with the imaginary heroine of Southerne's "pathetic" tragedy is attractive to the reader, as Tom's seeming indifference to the performance of *Hamlet* was not very attractive.[5]

But Sophia is made to seem somewhat absurd in her lack of control. It is not a tear that trickles down her lovely cheek, but "a Shower of Tears ran down into her Bosom," a description which, if visualized, is grotesque, surrealistic, and highly laughable. Such an exaggerated description would have been appropriate for a character like Mrs. Slipslop. The reader is not allowed time in which to laugh, however, for while Sophia weeps, illusion is replaced by "reality," and both literally and symbolically "the Book dropt from her Hand." Bookish distress gives way to real distress:

In this Situation she had continued a Minute, when the Door opened, and in came Lord *Fellamar. Sophia* started from her Chair at his Entrance; and his Lordship advancing forwards, and making a low Bow, said, " I am afraid Miss *Western,* I break in upon you abruptly." " Indeed my Lord," says she, " I must own myself a

---

[5] A. D. McKillop suggests the limitations of Fielding's method by remarking that in his presentation of Sophia " there is no emphasis on the divided mind . . . , and Sophia is never enveloped in an atmosphere of tragic melancholy, even though at the beginning of the attempted rape by Lord Fellamar she is found reading Southerne's *Fatal Marriage* (XV, v)."—*The Early Masters of English Fiction* (Lawrence, Kansas, 1956), p. 128.

little surprized at this unexpected Visit."—"If this Visit be un-expected Madam," answered Lord *Fellamar*, "my Eyes must have been very faithless Interpreters of my Heart, when last I had the Honour of seeing you : For surely you could not otherwise have hoped to detain my Heart in your Possession, without receiving a Visit from its owner." *Sophia*, confus'd as she was, answered this Bombast (and very properly, I think,) with a Look of inconceivable Disdain. My Lord then made another and a longer Speech of the Same Sort. Upon which *Sophia*, trembling said, "Am I really to conceive your Lordship to be out of your Senses? Sure, my Lord, there is no other Excuse for such Behaviour."—"I am, indeed, Madam, in the Situation you suppose," cries his Lordship; "and sure you will pardon the Effects of a Frenzy which you yourself have occasioned : For Love hath so totally deprived me of Reason, that I am scarce accountable for any of my Actions."—"Upon my Word, my Lord," said *Sophia*, "I neither understand your Words nor your Behaviour."—"Suffer me then, Madam," cries he, "at your Feet to explain both, by laying open my Soul to you, and declaring that I doat on you to the highest Degree of Distraction. O most adorable, most divine Creature! what Language can express the Sentiments of my Heart?"—"I do assure you, my Lord," said *Sophia*, "I shall not stay to hear any more of this."—"Do not," cries he, "think of leaving me thus cruelly : Could you know half the Torments which I feel, that tender Bosom must pity what those Eyes have caused." Then fetching a deep Sigh, and laying hold of her Hand, he ran on for some Minutes in a Strain which would be little more pleasing to the Reader, than it was to the Lady; and at last concluded with a Declaration, "That if he was Master of the World, he would lay it at her Feet." *Sophia* then forcibly pulling away her Hand from his, answered, with much Spirit, "I promise you, Sir, your World and its Master, I should spurn from me with equal Contempt." She then offered to go, and Lord *Fellamar* again laying Hold of her Hand, said, "Pardon me, my beloved Angel, Freedoms which nothing but Despair could have tempted me to take.—Believe me, could I have had any Hope that my Title and Fortune, neither of them incon-siderable, unless when compared with your Worth, would have been accepted, I had, in the humblest Manner, presented them to your Acceptance. — But I cannot lose you. — By Heaven, I will sooner part with my Soul. — You are, you must, you shall be only mine." — " My Lord," said she, " I intreat you to desist from a vain Pursuit; for, upon my Honour, I will never hear you on this Subject. Let go my Hand, my Lord, for I am resolved to go from you this Moment, nor will I ever see you more." — " Then, Madam," cries his Lordship, " I must make the best Use of this Moment; for I cannot, nor will live without you." — "What do you mean, my Lord?" said *Sophia*. " I will raise the Family."—" I have no Fear, Madam," answered he, " but of losing you, and that I am resolved to prevent, the only Way which Despair points to me." — he then caught her in his Arms; upon which she screamed so loud, that she must have alarmed some one to her Assistance, had not Lady *Bellaston* taken Care to remove all Ears.

If "poor" Sophia thinks that she is alone with Lord Fellamar ("that odious Lord") during this dialogue, which otherwise might come from sophisticated stage-drama, she is mistaken; for Fielding, in the guise of comic author, sits at one side to protect her and to interpolate his observations. He allows his delightful heroine to "get by" with nothing in the way of self-pity or self-satisfaction. Just as he has smiled at her over-exuberant tears, now he smiles at her righteous look of disdain "(and very properly, I think)." A little later, pretending to spare the reader some of Fellamar's amatory declaration, Fielding interrupts to say that he is hastening the dialogue along. He clearly intends to keep Fellamar in his place.

The minuet-like pace and politeness of Fellamar's opening remarks are entertaining to the reader, who knows the Lord's dire intent but also knows how Lady Bellaston had overcome his reluctance only after emphasizing Sophia's charms and fortune, reminding him of Paris's rape of Helen and of the rape of the Sabine women, and by praising Tom Jones as "a Man of Spirit." Lord Fellamar is a reluctant rapist, but he has proceeded so far as to kiss Sophia's neck, disordering the bag of his wig in the struggle, when Sophia's father bursts in upon the scene.

When the book fell from her hand, Sophia had abandoned herself to tears inspired by vicissitudes of an imaginary character, one intended for the stage. But she meets her own vicissitudes with dignity and patience, not finally screaming for aid until violence is offered. Shamela, when Mr. Booby made amorous attempts, liked to scream and pretended to faint away, in order to fool him into thinking her respectable. Sophia, who is eminently respectable, does not faint away but struggles when reasoning with Lord Fellamar proves useless. Her emotional tears are reserved for the feigned suffering in *The Fatal Marriage,* not for the scene with Fellamar, which perhaps seems less "real" to her than the scene of Isabella's disposing of her wedding ring. By having the book drop from Sophia's hand, to be replaced by experience, Fielding seems to comment amusingly on the nature of reality. If, as Bishop Berkeley thought, all existence is a mental act, willed by a perceiving mind, the world of imagination may be more "real" than the world of experienced events. By discrediting one kind of fiction, Fielding makes his own fiction seem more convincing.

VIII

Some Minute Wheels

Tom Jones

*The World may indeed be considered as a vast Machine,
in which the great Wheels are originally set in Motion by
those which are very minute, and almost imperceptible
to any but the strongest Eyes.—Tom Jones, V, iv.*

For appreciation of *Tom Jones,* more than for Fielding's earlier
fiction, the reader must see how objects and images function both
literally and symbolically, and he must watch the play of language
in action. Among the devices contributing to the novel's "system
of actions" are (1) ironic variations on the theme of "prudence,"
(2) a recurring analogy of food and love, (3) a cycle of clothes
images, (4) a consciously altering pattern of "bitch" references,
and (5) Sophia Western's muff. All of them assist with the feigning of "reality."

PRUDENCE

With even more shifts of meaning than "good" and "great"
suffer in *Jonathan Wild,* "decency," "honor," "love," "wisdom,"
"prudence," and other abstract nouns in *Tom Jones* are diverted
from their central, denotative, positive moral meaning. By means
of amusing devices that might be called "rhetorical betrayal,"
"contextual contamination," "dialectic undermining," and "ambiguous display," Fielding tampers indefatigably with "prudence"

until the reader is forced into a reconsideration of the true meaning of the word.

William Empson describes the style in *Tom Jones* as predominantly a "double irony." By this he means the ironist's ambiguous phrasing which allows both the reader and the target of the irony to think, "He is secretly on my side, and only pretends to sympathize with the other," while in truth the ironist "may hold some wise balanced position between them, or contrariwise may be feeling 'a plague on both your houses.'"[1] But, as I think Mr. Empson would be the first to agree, the irony is often many-bodied rather than merely double. And I think Mr. Empson would also agree that the ironic inquiries into moral ambiguities in *Tom Jones* are almost invariably infused with a tolerant, comic sweetness quite unlike the relatively nagging, shrill tone in *Jonathan Wild*.

The treatment of "prudence," for instance. It is the one good quality noticeably lacking in Tom's character; without it he cannot be a completely good man; and in the structure of the novel its absence prevents him from discovering his true identity, receiving recognition for his worth, and coming into his own. Exactly because it is indispensable to Tom's salvation and because it is no easy thing to achieve, "prudence" is subjected to the severest ironic alterations. Fielding turns it this way and that to alienate it from its good context, associating it with minds or actions that are hypocritical, mean, or grasping. All the despicable characters in the novel are "prudent" but do not approach Tom's state of partial goodness *without* "prudence."

Allworthy exhorts Tom to add "prudence" to his other good qualities (V, vii); imprudence leads Tom into his lowest fortunes; but finally we are told that Tom has acquired "Prudence very uncommon in one of his lively Parts" (XVIII, xii). This is a staple theme in didactic or "educational" fiction; twenty-five

---

[1] William Empson, "Tom Jones," *Kenyon Review*, XX (Spring, 1958), 218–219.

years before *Tom Jones* was published, Eliza Haywood began her *Idalia* ("A Novel") by inquiring "If there were a Possibility that the Warmth and Vigour of Youth cou'd be Temper'd with a due Consideration, and the Power of judging rightly, how easy were it to avoid the Ills which most of us endure? How few would be unhappy?" And "prudence" was urged as a rule of conduct in John Mason's *Self-Knowledge* (1745), Soame Jenyns's *The Modern Fine Gentleman* (a satire, 1746), *The Rule of Life* (3rd ed. 1747), and David Hartley's *Observations on Man* (Preface dated 1748). The difference in *Tom Jones* results from Fielding's breadth of vision, energy, and comic sense of truth. He employs "prudence" in his novel less often straightforwardly than in a betrayed, contaminated, or undermined sense; and true "prudence" endures all the teasing and testing.

In her valuable essay on "prudence" in *Tom Jones,* Eleanor Newman Hutchens shows how the first appearance of the term, in connection with Bridget Allworthy, is typical of Fielding's method.[2] Miss Bridget "very rightly conceived the Charms of Person in a Woman to be no better than Snares for herself, as well as for others, and yet so discreet was she in her Conduct, that her Prudence was as much on guard, as if she had all the Snares to apprehend which were ever laid for her whole Sex" (I, ii). Although Fielding causes Miss Bridget to appear ridiculous in this passage, he is by no means portraying her ironically as *im*prudent; he assigns to her a "prudence" of self-conscious officiousness, prudery, and careful appearance of virtuousness. It is "prudence" without value. Irony is further enforced by one's amused deduction that Squire Allworthy's old-maid sister is endowed with insufficient charms to make all her guards worthwhile. But, as Eleanor Newman Hutchens points out, this is only Fielding's irony in half light; for one finally learns in Book XVIII that Miss Bridget's guards had indeed proved insufficient, that

---

[2] Eleanor Newman Hutchens, essay, scheduled for publication in *Philological Quarterly,* October, 1960.

she had been caught in snares of the flesh, and that her real "prudence" lay in her discreetly protecting her reputation by never admitting she bore the bastard Tom. This is "double irony," not in Mr. Empson's terms necessarily, but because it functions twice, in a surprising new guise when it reappears after the delay of hundreds of pages, accreting significance along the way.

An especially varied irony infuses the word "prudent" in one passage cited by Miss Hutchens. It concerns a landlord who has lost a silver spoon and is in perpetual fear that his inn will be robbed. When the landlord at first apologizes to Tom because his wife has locked up almost all his possessions, Fielding interpolates information for the reader that the wife has that morning "almost stript the poor Man of all his Goods, as well as Money," to set up her favorite daughter in housekeeping. He has no goods to protect; but becoming suspicious of Tom he attempts to sit up all night to prevent a possible theft :

In reality, he might have been very well eased of these Apprehensions by the prudent Precautions of his Wife and Daughter, who had already removed every thing which was not fixed to the Freehold . . . (VII, x).

Although "prudence" benefiting the landlord was not the motive behind their stripping the house, this act of the mother and daughter, as Miss Hutchens says, "has the effect of securing the landlord against robbery, as much as if prudence had dictated the action. On the other hand, he is deprived of his goods as effectually as if he had been robbed. So the depredations of the wife and daughter are seen comically as bringing about a situation which might have resulted equally from prudence or imprudence (making oneself liable to robbery) but which actually results from neither."[3] But in the context of the novel the ironic

---

[3] *Ibid.;* and her "Verbal Irony in *Tom Jones,*" unpubl. diss., Univ. of Pennsylvania (1957), p. 75.

reference to "prudent Precautions" of a daughter is widely suggestive. At the landlord's inn with Tom is a Quaker, ironically described as an "honest, plain" man, whose daughter has eloped against his wishes; he tells how he "locked her up carefully," how she escaped to marry "the Lover of her own choosing," and how he has taken precautions to disown her forever. Tom, hearing this, is so strongly reminded of Squire Western's "prudent Precautions" of locking Sophia away from him, that he shouts at the Quaker, stares wildly, and pushes him out of the room. False or inapplicable "prudence" in a variety of references controls the whole passage.

A full analysis of style in *Tom Jones* would have to take into consideration the occasional purple passages, the fun with mock-heroics, the manipulation of rhythm and pause, the sometimes elaborate but generally unobtrusive parallels, and the marriage of formal and colloquial modes hardly to be found elsewhere in English fiction. But surely the most important item of style is Fielding's absolute control over verbal irony. It was this, I think, that Allen Tate meant when he spoke of the undeviating "bright level" and "beautiful tone" in *Tom Jones*—an achievement of style "like a man walking a tight rope" without ever slipping. It must have been this daring, tight-rope-walking control over verbal irony that William Empson described by saying that "When Fielding goes really high in *Tom Jones* his prose is like an archangel brooding over mankind . . . ."[4]

2. THE APPETITES

In his metaphorical cliché of "appetite" to discriminate between lust and love, Fielding suggestively conjoins plot, characterization, and moral theme in *Tom Jones*. He employs serious

---

[4] Allen Tate, "Fielding—*Tom Jones*," *The New Invitation to Learning,* ed. Mark Van Doren (New York, 1942), p. 203; William Empson, *op. cit.,* p. 222.

wit to expose or dramatize certain "hungers," significant in the story, of Allworthy, Captain Blifil, young Blifil, Tom, Mrs. Waters, and Sophia Western. Furthermore, both the author and reader themselves are involved.

In the opening chapter, a "Bill of Fare to the Feast," Fielding promises to serve up Human Nature in all its variety, "as difficult to be met with in Authors, as the *Bayonne* Ham or *Bologna* Sausage is to be found in the Shops." Human Nature, including love, he says, is no simple, single thing. Another introductory chapter, to Book VI, distinguishes at length between the benevolent disposition of true love and "the Desire of satisfying a voracious Appetite with a certain Quantity of delicate white human Flesh." The latter is the hunger of the glutton who "LOVES such and such Dishes" or "HUNGERS after such and such Women." Preparing here for Tom Jones's defection with Molly Seagrim, Fielding ironically suggests that the reader's own idea of love is perhaps that of "a Dish of Soup, or a Sirloin of Roast-beef."

Squire Allworthy, Tom's guardian, had married a beautiful woman for true love, but now as a benevolent widower he "hungers after Goodness" which, when "thoroughly satisfied," affords him repose more pleasing than that "occasioned by any other hearty Meal . . ." (I, iii). And, acting benevolently, Allworthy allows each person at his table to "satisfy all his Appetites within the Restrictions of Law, Virtue and Religion . . ." (I, x). Sharing the freedom of this table, Captain Blifil marries Allworthy's old-maid sister Bridget; for, "having a very good Appetite, and but little Nicety, he fancied he should play his Part very well at the matrimonial Banquet, without the Sauce of Beauty" (I, xi). Their offspring, the despicable young Blifil, though not wishing to "eat every Woman he saw," felt his animal appetite directed toward Sophia Western ("a most delicious Morsel"), experiencing "the same Desires which an Ortolan inspires into the Soul of an Epicure" (VII, vi).

Although Tom's love for Sophia certainly does not exclude the animal appetite, it is benevolent. Separated from her, Tom is enraptured to think that she may have her eyes "fixed on that very Moon which I behold at this Instant!" But his companion, Partridge, unromantically prefers to have his eyes "fixed on a good Sirloin of Roast Beef . . ." (VIII, ix). Later, despite a "Neglect of Food" caused by his love for the absent Sophia, Tom is prompted by Partridge to attack a serving of bacon and eggs "as heartily and voraciously as *Partridge* himself." Similarly, says Fielding, "place a good Piece of well-powdered Buttock before a hungry Lover, and he seldoms fails very handsomely to play his Part" (XII, v). In an earlier work Fielding had employed this same memorable but indelicate metaphor to show how sexual love on the level of mere appetite is like the eucharistic love-appetite "a lusty Divine is apt to conceive for the well-drest Sirloin, or handsome Buttock, which the well-edified 'Squire, in Gratitude, sets before him . . ." (*Jonathan Wild*, II, viii).

Tom's crucial defection with Mrs. Waters is presented almost entirely in terms of "appetite" and "hunger." While Tom concentrates upon his beef and ale, his person is lustfully ogled by Mrs. Waters, who "could feast heartily at the Table of Love, without reflecting that some other already had been, or hereafter might be, feasted with the same Repast." Placing herself before Tom, she smiles, ogles, and flatters in a fashion not intended to gain access merely to "an excellent Sirloin of Beef, or Bottle of *Burgundy*." Although her amorous glances at first, "hit only a vast Piece of Beef" on the table and her sighs are drowned by the "coarse Bubbling of some bottled Ale," she does succeed in engaging not only Tom's attention but his body as well to satisfy her greedy appetite (IX, vi).

In *Jonathan Wild* Fielding had written ironically of modern London cannibalism in "those Eating-Houses in *Covent-Garden,* where female Flesh is deliciously drest and served up to the greedy Appetites of young Gentlemen . . ." (II, ix). Sophia Western finds that in London an attractive, wealthy girl is hunted like a doe, probably to be "at last devoured" (XVII, iv).

Sophia escapes that fate, of course, and is joined with Tom in a union characterized by love that combines healthy appetite with tender benevolence and mutual esteem. In his final chapter Fielding tells us that Sophia "officiated as the Mistress of Ceremonies, or, in the polite Phrase, did the Honours of the Table. She had that Morning given her Hand to Jones . . . ." Theirs is a mutual appetite refined. As J. Middleton Murry succinctly and accurately puts the final relationship of Tom and Sophia, "This consummation of physical passion between a man and a woman of good nature who love one another, Fielding holds, very definitely, to be the supreme felicity attainable on earth." [5]

3. CLOTHES

Tom Jones's history can be followed through a series of vestments and divestments, from his first appearance in coarse linen wrappings in Squire Allworthy's bed to the final announcement that he is "now completely dressed." [6] Allworthy's benevolence toward Tom is first manifested in his order for "proper Clothes" to be procured for the infant (I, iii); and even when he has followed Blifil's malicious advice to evict Tom, Allworthy sends his "Clothes and every thing else" after him (VI, xii). Nevertheless the rejection of Tom enters popular gossip in terms of the Squire's

---

[5] J. Middleton Murry, " In Defence of Fielding," *Unprofessional Essays* (London, 1956), p. 36. Three years after the publication of *Tom Jones*, Fielding wittily redefined the confusion of values from which Tom and Sophia escaped: "LOVE. A Word properly applied to our Delight in particular Kinds of Food; sometimes metaphorically spoken of the favourite Objects of all our *Appetites*."—" A Modern Glossary," *The Covent-Garden Journal*, No. 4, 14 January, 1752.

[6] Dorothy Van Ghent remarks on a recurring " buried clothes metaphor " by which Fielding in *Tom Jones* intends to distinguish between appearances and reality, as in " that Colour of Sadness in which she dressed her Person and Countenance " (II, ix).—*The English Novel: Form and Function* (New York, 1953), p. 323.

having "stripped him stark naked . . . . Turned naked out of Doors!" (VI, xiii; VIII, viii). When Tom considers joining some soldiers on an expedition, an unsympathetic landlord remarks that he "shall wear a laced Waistcoat truly" (VII, xi). But even in his ordinary clothes Tom is a handsome youth, and when he "walked down-stairs neatly dressed, . . . perhaps the fair *Adonis* was not a lovelier Figure" — at least in the smitten opinion of Nanny the chambermaid (VIII, iv). Tom evidently possesses a considerable stock of linen, for when he leaves everything else behind in Partridge's house his "few Shirts" packed for the road are eight in number (VIII, vii). On the road Tom is significantly described by a rumor-mongering pettifogger as a bastard who has been "bred up, and fed, and clothified all to the World like any Gentleman . . ." (VIII, viii).

Can Tom the Foundling, now rejected by the benevolent hand that clothed him like a country gentleman, prove his right to be "clothified" in a gentleman's apparel? In London, seeking Sophia, he is conspicuously out of fashion : dressed in a "Suit of Fustian" and with a cheap-handled sword at his side, he receives only surly answers from a porter through whom he hopes to get news of Sophia. When her cousin Mrs. Fitzpatrick does condescend to receive him, his natural parts cause her to overlook his unostentatious dress :

There is a certain Air of natural Gentility, which it is neither in the Power of Dress to give, nor to conceal. Mr. *Jones,* as hath been before hinted, was possessed of this in a very eminent Degree. He met, therefore, with a Reception from the Lady, somewhat different from what his Apparel seemed to demand; and after he had paid her his proper Respects, was desired to sit down. (XIII, ii)

This "Air of natural Gentility" in Tom, joined with his vigorous animal spirits, attracts the amorous attention of Lady Bellaston to his person. Significantly again, Tom is disguised in mask and domino — "a Dress which, at another Season, would have certainly raised a Mob at his Heels" — for his assignation with Lady Bellaston (XIII, vi). Unaware of her identity at first, he attended the masquerade at the Opera-house at her invitation in hopes of learning Sophia's whereabouts. Becoming Lady Bellaston's paid lover for a period of ten days or so, Tom is now in disguise indeed. Now we are told that "Mr. *Jones* was just dressed to wait on Lady *Bellaston*" (XIII, x); and she speaks of him as being "genteelly dressed" (XIII, xii). The "gaiety" of Tom's dress is remarked upon; and when Lady Bellaston has been spurned and is plotting Tom's ruin, she identifies him as a beggar and a vagabond who has "procured himself tolerable Clothes, and passed for a Gentleman" (XV, vii; XVI, vii). The fight in which Tom nearly becomes a murderer follows upon Fitzpatrick's seeing him as a "young well-dressed Fellow coming from his Wife" (XVI, x). The constable into whose custody he falls, "seeing Mr. *Jones* very well drest," treats him with civility (XVI, x). But the civility in deference to well-tailored London apparel is undeserved : the clothes are not truly Tom's but represent his servitude to Lady Bellaston. "By her Means he was now become one of the best dress'd Men about Town" (XIII, ix).

At the end, released from prison and from the accusations of murder and incest, aware of his real identity as Allworthy's nephew and reconciled with him, and about to be reunited with Sophia, Tom has "barely Time left to dress himself." Partridge assists him but is no less excited than his master, making "almost as many Mistakes while he was dressing *Jones,* as I have seen made by *Harlequin* in dressing himself on the Stage" (XVIII, xi). Then :

Jones being now completely dressed, attended his Uncle to Mr. *Western's*. He was indeed one of the finest Figures ever beheld, and his Person alone would have charmed the greater Part of Womankind; but we hope it hath already appeared in this History, that Nature, when she formed him, did not totally rely, as she sometimes doth, on this Merit only, to recommend her Work (XVIII, xii).

4. BITCH

In *Tom Jones* the character most strongly conceived and portrayed is not Tom Jones but his eventual father-in-law, the fox-hunting Jacobite, Squire Western. The Squire's speech, personal habits, obsessions, pig-headed family relationships, and public displays are realized in affectionate and memorable detail. Fielding's delight in building up his characterization, welding him vitally into the action, is discernible throughout every episode in which he appears. As Lionel Trilling says, "It is some sort of love that Fielding has for Squire Western that allows him to note the great, gross details that bring that insensitive, sentient being into existence for us." Western is indeed eccentric, gross, and verging upon caricature, but he is simultaneously more convincing as a human creature, more palpably threatening to roar out of the confining print on the page, than other characters in almost anybody else's fiction. Western is outrageously alive: "In Fielding," Wyndham Lewis wrote, "where satire in creative fiction has its beginning, as has the novel itself, the types are very near to life . . . . I cannot see that Squire Weston [sic] is other than a living country magnate of that time. If we could go back into that century, and live with such people for a while, they would behave identically — exploding into language bristling with the word 'Pox' . . . ."[7]

Western's bristling arguments, harangues, and outcries (in conjunction of course with Fielding's muscular exposition) are largely responsible for the mark he makes upon the reader's memory. Western shows himself capable, in some passages, of speaking English nearly as correct as that of Allworthy, but to gain his way and force his will upon everyone around him, he

---

[7] Lionel Trilling, "Manners, Morals, and the Novel," *The Liberal Imagination* (New York, 1950), pp. 216–217; Wyndham Lewis, *Rude Assignment* (London, 1950), p. 45. See also V. S. Pritchett, "The Tough School," *The Listener*, LI (20 May, 1954), on Western the "unreasonable natural man, the stud bull of country life" (862).

slides down into partial Somersetshire dialect, then into almost
unintelligible country speech, and then—if the situation is still
not in his control—into shouted vulgarities which are sometimes
accompanied by the appropriate gestures or noises. At one time
or another he employs the word "bitch" to express his opinion
of almost every other important person in the novel.

When Molly Seagrim bears a child and Western guesses Tom
to be its father, he cries out, "D––n un, what a sly B––ch 'tis"
(IV, x). He remarks that "*Allworthy* is a queer B––ch," that Tom
is a "Son of a Bitch," and that Miss Western, his own sister, is
"a Presbyterian *Hanoverian* B––––" (VI, i; VI, x; VII, v).
Vexed at the thought that he might be stricken out of his sister's
will, he "ejaculated twenty Bitches": "The Bitch can't live for
ever, and I know I am down for it upon the Will" (XVI, iv).
Trapped away from his drinking and hunting cronies in "a whole
Room-full of Women," he terms them "a Kennel of Hoop-
petticoats B––––s," and he singles out Lady Bellaston as "that
fat a-se B––––" (XVII, iii). Rather than be set upon by a pack
of females, he says in the same passage, he would "rather be run
by my own Dogs, as one *Acton* was, that the Story Book says, was
turned into a Hare; and his own Dogs kill'd un, and eat un."

After shouting a hunting hollo, Western laments pathetically
that most men are "*whipt in* by the Humours of some d––nd
B–––– or other." Just as his sister who now torments him is a
bitch, his dead wife was a bitch during their married life. "Was
not thy Mother a d–––d B–––– to me? Answer me that," he
says to Sophia (VII, iv; VII, v).

Besides his hunting dogs only one companion has any sentimental hold on Western's heart, and that is his daughter Sophia.
Expecting her, like the dogs, to be obedient, provide entertainment for him, and appreciate his affection, he does not much
distinguish between dogs and daughter, wanting them all to be
around him:

Mr. *Western* grew every Day fonder and fonder of *Sophia,* inso-
much that his beloved Dogs themselves almost gave Place to her
in his Affections; but as he could not prevail on himself to abandon
these, he contrived very cunningly to enjoy their Company, together
with that of his Daughter, by insisting on her riding a-hunting with
him (IV, xiii).

Sophia dutifully complies; and it is when she is thrown from
her hunting horse that Tom rescues her. Thus Western's love for
his dogs and daughter leads indirectly to the certainty of Sophia
and Tom that they are in love.

More than half way through the novel, at the Upton inn,
"bitch" is applied to Sophia herself when Western thinks he has
caught her with Tom : "As soon as *Western* saw *Jones,* he set up
the same Holla as is used by Sportsmen when their Game is in
View. He then immediately run up and laid hold of *Jones,* crying,
'We have got the Dog Fox, I warrant the Bitch is not far off'"
(X, vii). Western's ensuing pursuit of his daughter is diverted by a
pack of running hounds and his joining the chase, "one of the
finest he ever saw." When Western spurs his horse on, crying
"She's gone, she's gone! Damn me if she is not gone!" he refers
to the fox bitch and not to Sophia whom he has temporarily for-
gotten (XII, ii). Later, tracking her down at Lady Bellaston's
house in London, he makes the house ring with his shouts of
"Where is she? D––n me, I'll unkennel her this Instant"; and
then, when she refuses to consider Blifil as a husband, he takes
hold of her hand violently and refers to her as an "undutiful
B––––" (XV, v). Like a stubborn dog that will not obey her
master's orders, Sophia displeases her father.

In London Squire Western reverts more often to country
dialect, coarseness, and hunting language than he did in Somersetshire. He admits to his sister that he "can't be expected to
know much of the Streets and the Folks" in the city; what he
does know is "the Management of a Pack of Dogs, or the finding
a Hare sitting . . ." (XV, vi). Although his love for Sophia is

genuine and deep, he seems unable to address or manage her except in the language and the manner of the kennel. Thinking that she will at last accept Blifil in marriage, he encourages her to speak : "'Why wout ask, *Sophy?*' cries he, 'when dost know that I had rather hear thy Voice than the Music of the best Pack of Dogs in *England.* — Hear thee, my dear little Girl! I hope I shall hear thee as long as I live . . .'" (XVI, ii). But this expression of love, accompanied by tears, is followed by fury when Sophia remains adamant and will not accede to his paternal commands.

Just before the discovery that Tom is Allworthy's nephew and heir, and when Sophia vows that if she does not marry Tom she will never marry, she is still "the little B————" in her father's opinion. He tells Allworthy that he will return her to Somersetshire, lock her in a garret, and allow her nothing to eat but bread and water (XVIII, viii). Allworthy's patient arguments for confidence in Sophia and for kindness in governing her do not impress Western. But after the reversal in Tom's fortunes, "No sooner than was *Western* informed of Mr. *Allworthy's* Intention to make *Jones* his Heir, than he joined heartily with the Uncle in every Commendation of the Nephew, and became as eager for her Marriage with *Jones,* as he had before been to couple her to *Blifil*" (XVIII, ix).

And now Western's hearty, coarse enthusiasm for the marriage and its consummation is in terms of the kennel and chase : he cries out in "his hunting Voice and Phrase," "To her, Boy, to her, go to her.————That's it, little Honeys. O that's it" (XVIII, xii).

With delicate irony Fielding appends the information that now old Western, mellowed by time and experience but still essentially unchanged, has a granddaughter "of whom the old Gentleman is so fond, that he spends much of his time in the Nursery, where he declares the Tattling of his little Grand-Daughter, who is above a Year and a half old, is sweeter Music than the finest Cry of Dogs in *England*" (XVIII, xiii). Writing to Esther Johnson, Jonathan Swift once affectionately concluded a letter with the words, "Agre[e]able B–tch," a term Western would now contentedly apply to Sophia and her child.[*]

It is of course only one of the devices through which Squire Western's strong characterization comes clear; but throughout the novel his varied use of "bitch" and his confusion of dogs and daughter are on almost every occasion intimately tied up with the unfolding story, the deepening of other characterizations as well as Western's, and the moral themes Fielding is interested in placing entertainingly before the reader.

5. SOPHIA WESTERN'S MUFF

Sophia's muff is one of the most entertaining devices in *Tom Jones*, vital in a series of widening actions, assisting with characterization, and implying relationships that would be falsified if openly stated. It is a means by which Fielding suggests states of mind and emotion that could not very well have been merely explicated or dramatized, partly because they are — at first, anyhow — states that the characters themselves do not fully recognize.

Because it represents, among other things, physical attraction between Tom and Sophia, the muff is not introduced (indeed may be said not to exist) until the pair are of marriageable age. Then it is introduced into the story casually, with no hint of its later importance, in Mrs. Honour's report of Tom's affection for her mistress:

"Why, Ma'am," answered Mrs. *Honour*, "he came into the Room, one Day last Week when I was at Work, and there lay your Ladyship's Muff on a Chair, and to be sure he put his Hands into it, that very Muff your Ladyship gave me but yesterday; La, says I, Mr. *Jones*, you will stretch my Lady's Muff and spoil it; but he still kept his Hands in it, and then he kissed it — to be sure, I hardly ever saw such a Kiss in my Life as he gave it." (IV, xiv)

---

[*] Jonathan Swift, *Journal to Stella,* 6 June, 1713; and see William Empson on "Dog" in English literature and speech, *The Structure of Complex Words* (London, 1951), pp. 158–184.

This anecdote is preceded by Mrs. Honour's characterization
of Tom as sweet-tempered, popular, and gentlemanly, with "the
whitest Hands in the World," and is followed by her assurance
of Tom's affection, which has never been expressed to Sophia.
Thus, through the muff (a substitute for the actual object of his
affections), both Sophia and the reader first learn of Tom's true
feelings and wishes.

Again with Mrs. Honour as intermediary, or Messenger, and
the muff as evidence, a companion-scene allows Tom to learn of
Sophia's love for him. In conversation with Tom, Mrs. Honour
lets him know that Sophia, upon learning of his association with
the muff, wished it again in her possession. Mrs. Honour characterizes Sophia attractively, assures Tom of her love, and says of
the muff, "'I believe, she hath worn it upon her Arm almost ever
since, and I warrants hath given it many a Kiss when nobody
hath seen her'" (V, iv). If Mrs. Honour can be believed, both
Tom and Sophia have made the muff a substitutional device
which receives their affection.

But still another scene involving the muff moves Tom from
amorousness to certainty of love. Tom and Squire Western listen
together, one evening, to Sophia at the harpsichord:

Sophia looked this Evening with more than usual Beauty; and
we may believe it was no small addition to her Charms, in the Eye
of Mr. *Jones,* that she now happened to have on her Right Arm this
very Muff.

She was playing one of her Father's favourite Tunes, and he was
leaning on her Chair, when the Muff fell over her Fingers, and put
her out. This so disconcerted the Squire, that he snatched the Muff
from her, and with a hearty Curse threw it into the Fire. *Sophia*
instantly started up, and with the utmost Eagerness recovered it
from the Flames. (V, iv)

An intermediary like Mrs. Honour is no longer required: the
muff now functions as an immediate tie between Tom and Sophia
—though there has still been no open profession of love verbally

between them. This scene, in which Fielding handles symbolism with careful complexity, widens the significance of the muff-device : the reader senses that, in the idyllic scene of Sophia's playing the harpsichord, Tom's eye is upon her muff; certainly Sophia, who insists upon wearing it during her filial performance at the keyboard, though it interferes with her playing, is self-conscious of what the muff means to Tom as well as to her. Squire Western, now first involved with the device, reveals by his gesture of throwing the muff into the fire that he does not wish to have his pleasure or his daughter taken from him. The conflict of muff and music results from Sophia's effort to have both : love of Tom and love of Western. But the two are irreconcilable, for Western will not accept Tom, and Tom will not violate Western's hospitality; his rejection is foreshadowed by the muff's being flung into the fire because it interferes with an act of daughterly devotion. Similarly, Sophia's retrieving the muff, at risk to herself, represents her determination to persist in love of Tom and foreshadows her escape from home. Tom, observing Sophia's impetuous action, abandons all reservations : "The Citadel of *Jones* was now taken by Surprize. All those Considerations of Honour and Prudence, which our Heroe had lately with so much military Wisdom placed as Guards over the Avenues of his Heart, ran away from their Posts, and the God of Love marched in in Triumph." Both Sophia and Tom are committed. The reader is led to believe, through the non-verbal vows evoked by means of the muff, that the love of the pair will somehow be realized before the last page of the novel is reached.

The muff next appears, as Sophia's substitute for Tom's person, when he has been turned out of Paradise Hall and has left Somersetshire. With ironic sympathy Fielding shows her weeping over the muff and over Tom's letter to her, her sole mementos of him, as though they could share her sorrow and loneliness (VII, v).

That scene is soon followed by another, more important episode which furthers the plot and characterizes Sophia (as well as presenting some of Fielding's ideas on love and human nature). It is the episode in which the muff, or what it represents — "the Thoughts of her beloved *Jones,* and some Hopes (however distant) in which he was very particularly concerned" — prevents Sophia from accepting the despised Blifil's offer of marriage, even when she is tempted out of self pity and respect for her father's wishes : "*Sophia* was charmed with the Contemplation of so heroic an Action, and began to compliment herself with much premature Flattery, when *Cupid,* who lay hid in her Muff, suddenly crept out, and, like *Punchinello* in a Puppet-shew, kicked out all before him" (VII, ix). Sophia is here depicted as the good daughter, and faithful to her true love, but a girl human enough to flirt with the self-satisfaction that would accompany martyring herself to parental commands. The muff, acting as a reminder of where her real affections lie, not in "filial Love, Piety, and Pride," but in desire for a lasting union with Tom, leads Sophia to defy her father and audaciously leave her home and all security behind her.

The four appearances of the muff rehearsed in the preceding paragraphs are set in the country, in Somersetshire. With both Tom and Sophia now on the road, the next four appearances, in a cluster, are set in the inn at Upton. Here the muff again is directly instrumental in the action : altering the plans of both Tom and Sophia; releasing information that intensifies, reverses, or introduces opinions for the reader as well as for the characters; and pressing the plot along. And the muff significantly shifts from Sophia's possession into Tom's.

First of the four Upton incidents is that in which Sophia, learning that Tom shares the bed of Mrs. Waters, has the muff placed in his empty bed. She departs, knowing that through this circumstance "Mr. *Jones* would be acquainted with her having been at the Inn, in a Way, which, if any Sparks of Affection for her remained in him, would be some Punishment, at least, for his

Faults" (X, v). Our muff-device becomes the means by which
Tom learns that Sophia has been seeking him; but he learns this
simultaneously knowing that she is aware of his defection with
another woman. We were earlier told that Sophia wept over the
muff; this passage tells us that it has become her bedfellow and
bodily substitute for Tom. For Sophia, the muff can be the
recipient of indignation and disappointment as well as of affection when, learning of Mrs. Waters, she somewhat revises her
attitude toward Tom. With all this in mind, Fielding entertainingly invites his reader to reconsider the uses of the muff thus far
and to watch for the device as it will be further engaged in the
action :

> The Reader will be pleased to remember a little Muff, which hath
> had the Honour of being more than once remembered already in
> this History. This Muff, ever since the departure of Mr. *Jones,* had
> been the constant companion of *Sophia* by Day, and her Bedfellow
> by Night; and this Muff she had at this very Instant upon her Arm;
> whence she took it off with great Indignation, and having writ her
> Name with her Pencil upon a Piece of Paper, which she pinned to
> it, she bribed the Maid to convey it to the empty Bed of Mr. *Jones,*
> in which, if he did not find it, she charged her to take some Method
> of conveying it before his Eyes in the Morning. (X, v)

In the next scene at Upton, Tom makes the unhappy discoveries which were foreshadowed by the account of Sophia's
decisions. Returning to his own bed before dawn, Tom had not
noticed the muff but had knocked it to the floor. When it attracts
his attention, a flood of knowledge and emotion is set loose :
"The Muff was so very remarkable, that our Heroe might
possibly have recollected it without the Information annexed. But
his Memory was not put to that hard Office, for at the same
Instant he saw and read the words *Sophia Western* upon the
Paper which was pinned to it. His Looks now grew frantic in a
Moment, and he eagerly cried out, 'Oh Heavens! how came this
Muff here!'" (X, vi).

Convinced of the true situation, Tom rushes into the kitchen of the inn, vainly hoping to apprehend Sophia, and there encounters Squire Western making inquiries after his daughter — "when *Jones* entered the Room, unfortunately having *Sophia*'s Muff in his Hand." Guessing that Tom has abducted his daughter ("'We have got the Dox Fox, I warrant the Bitch is not far off'"), Western is convinced by the sight of the muff that Sophia has been undone. "'My daughter's Muff !' cries the Squire, in a Rage. 'Hath he got my Daughter's Muff ! Bear Witness, the Goods are found upon him. I'll have him before a Justice of Peace this Instant. Where is my Daughter, Villain?'" (X, vii). For Western, "Hath he got my Daughter's Muff !" equates with "Hath he lain with my daughter!" The punishment intended by Sophia has been increased; for not only does Tom reproach himself, but he must endure Western's abuse. Western himself enters the angry pursuit that terminates, after an interruption, with the famous scene of his bursting in upon Sophia and the preposterous Lord Fellamar at Lady Bellaston's.

Finally, in a parody of law procedure based upon the felony of "Muff-stealing," the episodes at the inn are resolved with the muff accidentally left in Tom's possession. Giving everyone a hearty curse, Western orders his horses and sets off from the inn in pursuit of Sophia, so outraged that he neglects to take the muff from Tom, who "would have died on the Spot rather than have parted from it" (X, vii).

And now, like the symmetrical order of the novel itself (composed of a triptych with six books laid in the country, six on the road, and six in London, returning full circle to the country at the end), or like the introduction of the muff first to reveal Tom's affection and then Sophia's, there is an exact parallel to Sophia's employment of the muff as a substitute for the absent person. Just as she had made it her bedfellow in Tom's absence, so he, now that the muff has changed hands into his keeping, sleeps with it and another item that belonged to her. On the road to

London, in search of Sophia, he "retired to Rest, with his two Bed-fellows the Pocket-Book and the Muff" (XII, vi).

Again with symmetrical design the muff is instrumental in Tom's refusal of an offer of marriage in London : eight books earlier it had been the decisive factor in Sophia's refusal to marry Blifil. Mrs. Hunt's proposal is unquestionably attractive, for it offers Tom an eager widow, her fortune, and security; but he writes to her that his true affections are elsewhere. "When our Heroe had finished and sent this Letter, he went to his Scrutoire, took out Miss *Western*'s Muff, kiss'd it several Times, and then strutted some Turns about his Room with more Satisfaction of Mind than ever any *Irishman* felt in carrying off a Fortune of fifty Thousand Pounds" (XV, xi).

As an actively functioning device, the muff is past usefulness when it is for the last time referred to in the penultimate book, in Tom's summary for Mrs. Waters of "several Facts of which she was ignorant, as the Adventure of the Muff, and other Particulars, concealing only the Name of *Sophia*" (XVII, ix). Here the reference to the muff is followed immediately by Tom's avowal of intention to alter his way of living, lamenting "the Follies and Vices of which he had been guilty." The muff is a reminder of follies such as the one at the inn, assisted by Mrs. Waters, which caused him to lose Sophia there (thus setting the novel off on a pattern it would not otherwise have known). The muff — as article of apparel and as token — can be dispensed with; for Tom is soon to have Sophia herself, and no substitution-device is now necessary. Through the muff Fielding has amusingly drawn attention to states of mind and emotion which, though unformulated and uttered by the characters, impel them into important action or cause them to reject action, thus delineating the characters afresh while drawing the plot into new directions and enforcing the author's thought.

Sophia's muff was small (she wore it at the keyboard; and Partridge was trying to stuff it into his pocket when Tom saw it at the inn). Wrist-muffs or muffetees like Sophia's were sometimes of bright-colored fabrics, perhaps scarlet or Bremen blue and decorated with ribbons, and they were sometimes made of feathers; but they seem most often to have been of cony, sable, ermine, or some other fur.[9] The muff in *Tom Jones* is the lover's token from his lady, the scarf he wears as a knight on his travels, the source of strength in combat and reminder of commitment in scenes of temptation. Like Desdemona's strawberry-embroidered handkerchief or Fanny Price's necklace, it is somewhat differently interpreted by different characters and so becomes a source of misunderstandings as well as of understandings (for although the token soon· has a single meaning for Sophia and Tom, the meaning is only partly known to Mrs. Honour and not at all to Squire Western, Partridge, Parson Supple, and Mrs. Waters).

When Sophia's muff is scrutinized in this fashion, turned back and forth, and shaken to see what may be inside, it appears obvious enough as an amusing, deliberately half-concealed artifice. No one should complain that it has been "read into" the novel to satisfy a "modern" taste. Fielding himself, pausing in his story on the occasion of Sophia's rescuing her muff from the fire, self-consciously faces his reader to remark that although "this Incident will probably appear of little Consequence," it is from just such "little Circumstances" that "Events of the utmost Importance arise." He concludes, "The World may indeed be considered as a vast Machine, in which the great Wheels are originally set in Motion by those which are very minute, and almost imperceptible to any but the strongest Eyes" (V, iv). Thinking of the device in terms of "Incident" and "Circumstances," Fielding makes it inextricable from plot. Worked entertainingly into a series of incidents, it assumes heavy duties in the

---

[9] Eighteenth-century examples of the word " muff " under the heading of " Venery " may be found in Farmer and Henley, *Slang and Its Analogues Past and Present* (London, 1896), " Muff," Item 4.

novel's constructive art, the careful architecture and "perfect plot" for which *Tom Jones* has received praise. Such minute wheels belong prominently in the "system of actions" through which, as R. S. Crane says, a novel makes itself realized. As such a device, the muff does not perform in a fixed context, but expands and varies in meaning when it is re-introduced, accreting new significance during the progress of the novel. Propelling the plot along in a series of stages, it creates a somewhat intuitive view of the presented action.[10]

From Samuel Johnson's time to ours it has been conventional to speak of Fielding's "avoidance of the subjective dimension" and to repeat that his characters "do not have a convincing inner life." I have just quoted, not from Dr. Johnson, but from a very recent commentator on *Tom Jones.*[11] Perhaps the conventional idea of Fielding as a surface artist who was superb in "plot" but ostentatiously refused to probe into motives, can be somewhat minimized when it is seen to what extent he attempted — through the workings of minute wheels like the devices glanced at in this essay — to bring the inner life of his characters to view. *Tom Jones* can be read rewardingly with an eye precisely on techniques of

---

[10] A. D. McKillop, " Some Recent Views of *Tom Jones," College English,* XXI (October, 1959), 17–21, argues admirably that although Fielding " eschews detailed psychology and leans heavily on typical patterns of behavior," the effects of "the synthesis made by the author" are by no means without complexity and depth. Using the example of Sophia's muff, Mr. McKillop writes that " The historian's way is to display the importance of the incident of the muff, and moreover to remind us that this is exactly what he is doing. Thereafter the muff is more than a trivial cause or a prop—it is a symbol, and is supposed to speak for itself."

[11] Ian Watt, " Fielding as Novelist : ' Tom Jones,' " *The Rise of the Novel* (Berkeley and Los Angeles, 1957), p. 273. More judiciously and with reservations A. D. McKillop writes of Fielding's " comic externalization of character in action. . . . Here we have the great achievement but also the limitation of Fielding's art : the beautiful network of circumstance does not blend into the mysterious penumbra enveloping human action and human life "—*The Early Masters of English Fiction* (Lawrence, Kansas, 1956), p. 120.

narration usually associated with novelists who learned their art after the middle of the nineteenth century. Fielding utilizes the literary apparatus of illusion in order to dispel and transcend illusion. In 1749 he had pushed a considerable distance toward realization of Thomas Hardy's "visible essences" and Henry James's "representational values," "aspects," and "visibilities," through which theme, characters, and plot are subtly rendered.[12]

---

[12] See Howard O. Brogan, " ' Visible Essences ' in *The Mayor of Caster-bridge*," *ELH*, XVII (December, 1950), 307–323; and Henry James, Preface to *The Golden Bowl*, in *The Art of the Novel*, ed. R. P. Blackmur (New York, 1934), p. 346.

XI

The Noble Model

Amelia

"I do know your Meaning," cries the Doctor, "and Virgil
*knew it a great While ago. The next time you see your
Friend Mrs.* Atkinson, *ask her what it was made* Dido *fall
in Love with* Æneas." — *Amelia, XII, iii.*

In James Joyce's published letters one may read his advice,
addressed to his old aunt, to use the *Odyssey,* even in Lamb's
version for children, as a guide to understanding *Ulysses;* he
provided outline-keys for other correspondents, remarking that
his intention was "to transpose the myth *sub specie temporis
nostri"*; and in the Rosenbach Museum one may see the note-
books in which he wrote *Ulysses,* the sections headed in his nervous
calligraphy with reference to the corresponding *Odyssean* episodes. It has been argued that the true depth and scope of
Ulysses can be appreciated only after carefully working out the
parallels; but perhaps these parallels with the *Odyssey* should be
considered as a ladder to be kicked away and disregarded when
one has gained access to the work itself. But Joyce's consciously
elaborate method of transposition, never yet completely analyzed,
is unquestionable.[1]

Henry Fielding's *Amelia* (1751) is unquestionably patterned
upon the *Aeneid*; but beyond that statement I must confess that

---

[1] James Joyce, *Letters,* ed. Stuart Gilbert (New York, 1957), pp. 113, 145,
193.

the ground is mostly conjectural, with no manuscript or pertinent letters to offer assistance. A connection was acknowledged by Fielding himself, shortly after publication of *Amelia,* when he wrote defensively that this novel followed the rules for epic writing and "will be found to deviate very little from the strictest Observations of all those Rules; neither Homer nor Virgil pursued them with greater Care than myself, and the candid and learned Reader will see that the latter was the noble model, which I made use of on this Occasion."[2] This passage, when brought to Samuel Richardson's attention, did not tempt him to discover how Fielding had used "the noble model"—or perhaps he only pretended not to appreciate Fielding's artfully feigned imitation. To Lady Bradshaigh, Richardson wrote unpleasantly of his rival that "A person of honour asked me, the other day, what he could mean by saying, in his Covent-Garden Journal, that he had followed Homer and Virgil, in his Amelia. I answered, that he was justified in saying so, because he must mean Cotton's Virgil Travestied; where the women are drabs, and the men scoundrels."[3] As Richardson perfectly well knew, Fielding had Virgil, and not *Virgil Travestied,* in mind : *Amelia* may be considered a modern, domestic epic *sub specie temporis nostri,* following Virgil's *Aeneid,* within limits, in subject, characterization, and form. By bookishly reminding his reader of an ancient literary parallel, Fielding hopes to render his own fiction more "real" by comparison.

Whereas Virgil opened his poem seven years after Aeneas's escape from Troy, Fielding begins his novel seven years after Booth's marriage to Amelia. For both heroes these have been troubled, harried years, on sea and land, in wars and out of wars; and both men are, after further trials, to find their destinies and at last make their peace with heaven. Whereas Virgil sang of war

---

[2] Henry Fielding, *Covent-Garden Journal,* No. 8 (28 January, 1752).

[3] Samuel Richardson, 23 February, 1752, *Correspondence,* ed. Anna Barbauld (London, 1804), VI, 154–155.

and the travails of a great man, founder of a nation, Fielding
tells of "various Accidents which befel a very worthy Couple"
who try to establish a home for their children (six of them finally).
Where lay the cause of such calamities, and why should the gods
persevere in anger so relentlessly? Virgil asked at the outset.
Fielding in his *exordium* poses the same question, but must seek
an answer nearer home than in the malice of Fortune or the
grievances of the goddess Juno. Booth, a modern man, knows that
he is the victim of social injustices of his day, but he also largely
calls up his own troubles, by "quitting the Directions of Prudence,
and following the blind Guidance of a predominant Passion" :

The various Accidents which befel a very worthy Couple, after
uniting in the State of Matrimony, will be the Subject of the following History. The Distresses which they waded through, were some
of them so exquisite, and the Incidents which produced these so
extraordinary, that they seemed to require not only the utmost
Malice, but the utmost Invention which Superstition hath ever
attributed to Fortune : Tho' whether any such Being interfered in
the case, or, indeed, whether there be any such Being in the Universe,
is a Matter which I by no Means presume to determine in the
Affirmative. To speak bold Truth, I am, after much mature Deliber-
ation, inclined to suspect, that the Public Voice hath in all Ages
done much Injustice to Fortune, and hath convicted her of many
Facts in which she had not the least Concern. I question much,
whether we may not by natural Means account for the Success of
Knaves, and Calamities of Fools, with all the Miseries in which Men
of Sense sometimes involve themselves by quitting the Directions of
Prudence, and following the blind Guidance of a predominant
Passion; in short, for all the ordinary Phenomena which are imputed
to Fortune; whom, perhaps, Men accuse with no less Absurdity in
Life, than a bad Player complains of ill Luck at the Game of Chess.

But if Men are sometimes guilty of laying improper Blame on
this imaginary Being, they are altogether as apt to make her Amends,
by ascribing to her Honours which she as little deserves. To retrieve
the ill Consequences of a foolish Conduct, and by struggling man-
fully with Distress to subdue it, is one of the noblest Efforts of

Wisdom and Virtue. Whoever, therefore, calls such a Man fortunate, is guilty of no less Impropriety in Speech, than he would be, who should call the Statuary or the Poet fortunate, who carved *Venus,* or who writ an Iliad. (I, i)

Fielding thus neatly, amongst his moral observations and genial groundwork for introducing his characters and action, reminds the reader of the conscious artistry about to be experienced. Felicities in the story of Amelia and her husband, soon to be encountered, are painstakingly deliberate, no more accidental than a great poem or statue, or a good life fully lived. The reader is invited to consider *Amelia* as a planned work of art.[4]

As a study, not of warfare necessary to establish a nation, but of the vicissitudes of married life, *Amelia* has a double focus of interest in the wife and husband who, between them, possess some of Aeneas's characteristics which have been most remarked upon. His filial and national devotion (*pius Aeneas*) is represented by Amelia's unswerving conjugal devotion and affection; and Aeneas's inward weakness, requiring a struggle to act in the right direction, is represented first by Booth's trustful adult innocence, with which the reader cannot help sympathizing somewhat even when it is most irresponsible, and then by Booth's conviction "that a larger share of Misfortunes had fallen to his Lot than he had merited." Aeneas was assisted by Venus; Amelia assists herself and her husband by her own goodness, and the pair depends upon the long-suffering protection of Dr. Harrison and Sgt. Atkinson, who watch over Amelia through most of her trials.

George Sherburn tells us that "Fielding undertook in *Amelia* to write a sober, faithful history of his own times in humble prose — a history that yet should, in its structure, its organizing themes,

---

[4] But it is usually considered as something else, as " a pamphlet, a sermon, an indictment . . . . Apart from Mrs. Behn's *Oroonoko,* which scarcely counts, it is the first English novel of social reform, the first earnest study of actual conditions, with a clear lesson to propound and definite reforms to offer as a logical inference."—Ernest A. Baker, *The History of the English Novel* (London, 1930), IV, 159.

and in its pictures of domesticity, recall at least remotely the masterpiece of Vergil."[5] Like the *Aeneid*, Fielding's novel consists of twelve books. What follows below is its story in the light of its Virgilian source, a running account of the twelve book-divisions, isolating those points on which the two works seem to coincide. Of course, some important episodes and characters seem to hold no reminiscence of the *Aeneid*; such is Mr. Robinson, who first gives the vital information about Amelia's legacy, and such is the discovery of Amelia's gold-framed portrait. I have tried to limit myself to parallels which, after several readings, seem inescapable, restraining the impulse to draw fascinating but far-fetched connections.

BOOK I

Virgil's initial account of a storm at sea, the rescue, and the Trojans' arrival at Queen Dido's new capital is revised in terms of a London street altercation in which Booth tries to intercede, his arrest because he lacks money for a bribe, and his arrival in jail, where he will be entertained by Miss Matthews, whom he has not seen since his marriage to Amelia. The murder of Dido's husband, Sychaeus, by her brother Pygmalion, reappears here in the stabbing of Miss Matthews's consort, an Army officer named Hebbers, who has jilted her; her life, like Dido's, has been made miserable by a brother who treats her as "an inveterate Enemy." And her overture to Booth in the gift of a guinea, later followed by two more guineas, prosaically modernizes Dido's presentation to the Trojans of twenty bulls, a hundred lambs, and a hundred swine. Dido's feast in her Carthaginian palace, with which the first book of the *Aeneid* concludes, a matter of purple-upholstered couches and chieftains' toasts from a jeweled goblet, is diminished

---

[5] George Sherburn, "Fielding's *Amelia*: An Interpretation," *ELH*, III (March, 1936), 3. To Sherburn's essay, and to L. H. Powers, "The Influence of the *Aeneid* on Fielding's *Amelia*," *Modern Language Notes*, LXXI (May, 1956), 330–336, I am greatly indebted in this chapter.

to a prison meal and tea-table. Iopas's banquet song about the creation of the universe becomes "a facetious discourse," by a turn-key, a lawyer, Booth, Miss Matthews, and other prisoners, on the ethics of perjury. Like Aeneas when the meal is ended, Booth is urged to tell "what had befallen him."

BOOK II

In the second book Aeneas told of the end of Troy, and Booth tells of his wooing of Amelia and marriage to her. Led by Destiny to escape his doomed city, Aeneas reluctantly left his wife Creusa behind him. When Booth's regiment is ordered to leave for service in Gibraltar, "Thoughts of leaving *Amelia,* in her present Condition [pregnancy], to Misery, perhaps to Death or Madness, were insupportable." Because it may be possible to avoid duty overseas by means of an exchange with another officer, Booth must choose between love and honor, as Aeneas did when Creusa's phantom urged him to flee, reminding him of his divine purpose.

BOOK III

Aeneas continued his story, chiefly for Dido's ears, down to his landing on the Carthaginian coast; Booth gives his history down to his arrest and imprisonment. As Aeneas's adviser, Father Anchises bade him hoist the Trojans' sails and trust to the Fates; as Amelia's spiritual adviser and friend, Dr. Harrison counsels Booth that his honor is at stake in going to Gibraltar : it is his duty to his king, his country, and his conscience. But just as Anchises, "best of fathers," died in Book III of the *Aeneid,* Dr. Harrison becomes temporarily alienated from the Booths and is described as "dead to us," leaving them "bereft not only of the best Companion in the World, but of the best Counsellor." Both the epic poem and the novel introduce a Sea-Piece in Book III, violent with tossing waves, sudden night, and flashes of fire; the steersman Palinurus almost gave all for lost, as does the captain of the *Lovely Peggy* as it passes the rock of Scilly before it sinks. Warned of their danger, Aeneas and his crew had barely managed to avoid foundering upon the rocks of Scylla and Charybdis. [Amelia eventually joins her husband abroad, and when they return to England with their children she tries to assist him with a farm procured for them by Dr. Harrison. It is a failure and Booth has now come alone to London to escape from his debts.]

BOOK IV

With Aeneas's adventures told, Dido felt herself amorously inflamed, and Miss Matthews, "flushing," invites Booth ("not absolutely a Joseph") to "sit up all Night" : almost frantic with desire she employs "every Art to soften, to allure, to win, to enflame." Virgil's account of the enchantment by the gods to bring the lovers together in a cave is echoed amusingly by Fielding when he describes the jailer, who for a fee places Booth and Miss Matthews together for the night, as "Governor of the enchanted Castle." According to Rumor, the affair in Carthage continued all winter; that in the London jail lasts seven days and nights. But just as Booth's conscience plagues him in "fits of Virtue," Mercury had appeared to Aeneas to remind him that he was neglecting his destiny by not pursuing the search for his own realm. Both heroes leave their shocked mistresses unceremoniously, Booth in the company of his Amelia, who has appeared in the prison as "a female Spectre, all pale and breathless." Miss Matthews learns of her imminent release from prison in a letter from her wealthy suitor "Damon," in reality Col. James, who had been one of Booth's fellow-officers; and some of the most vexing troubles in the novel arise from Col. James's anger when he learns of Booth's amatory success with Miss Matthews. King Iarba, a suitor for Dido's hand, upon learning of her scandalous dalliance, was similarly enraged.

Entirely without reference to their Virgilian model, Rebecca West has characterized these first four books of *Amelia* as "a *tour de force* which has never been surpassed," a "dazzling introduction" to the eight books which follow. Miss West is impressed by the tension created by the healthy animal instinctiveness of the handsome pair, separating them from their squalid prison surroundings, during Booth's long monologue which is, the reader senses, inevitably to be followed by the act of adultery. "Fielding conveys," as Miss West exactly phrases it, that this act "inflicts an injury on Billy Booth's marriage, but cannot touch its essence."[6]

BOOK V

The careers of Aeneas and Booth are now unfolded, both men attempting, against odds that seem hopeless, to strike roots, both of them acting again and again unwisely and dogged by the malice of the Fates. The long anniversary games held in Anchises's memory seem metamorphosed and concentrated into the fifth chapter of this book in *Amelia*, "Containing much Heroic Matter," which presents the duel of Booth and Col. Bath, who thinks he is defending the honor of his brother-in-law, Col. James, unaware that James's foundationless jealousy has been fanned by Miss Matthews. The slippery field of blood, in which Nisus fell, seems recreated in that area of Hyde Park "called the Field of Blood," where the Colonel falls wounded by Booth's sword. Aeneas's *fidus Achates* is reincarnated perhaps in the faithful Sgt. Atkinson, who has been the admirer of Amelia since childhood, an aide to Booth overseas, the rescuer of the Booths' son in Book IV, and who now figures largely in Book V, especially as the secret husband of Mrs. Bennet. A somewhat incredible Noble Lord, as degenerate as Atkinson is noble, whose special hobby is that of ruining married women, fixes his attentions upon

---

[6] Rebecca West, *The Court and the Castle* (New Haven, 1957), pp. 92, 93.

Amelia through the mediation of Mrs. Ellison, one of his creatures, and hopes that by sending Booth to the West Indies he can
gain access to Amelia. This Noble Lord seems to be Fielding's
version of Turnus, whose rivalry was used by Juno to threaten
Aeneas with loss of Lavinia and of Latium, her dowry.

BOOK VI

Amelia innocently meets the Noble Lord, plays ombre in his
company, almost is persuaded by Mrs. Ellison to attend a masquerade at Ranelagh where his Lordship is to attack her, and
accepts presents from his hand. An expensive gold watch, given
to one of Amelia's children, may be the Golden Bough which
serves Booth—informed of his Lordship's way with women—
as his passport into the black Underworld of jealousy and doubt.
Just as Pope's mock heroic device in *The Rape of the Lock* sent
Belinda down into the Cave of the Spleen, Fielding now has
Booth haunted by frightful dreams, tormented by suspicion, and
"possessed by this worst of Fiends," jealousy. It is the twenty-
guinea gold watch which, seen by Dr. Harrison, causes him to
withhold financial aid from the family and to encourage Murphy,
the bailiff, to take Booth to jail, this time for his debts. Suitably,
Mrs. Bennet, who has been one of the Noble Lord's victims, now
quotes from the *Aeneid* Dido's speech on the subject of adultery.
But when Booth begins to recover his confidence, it is Amelia
whom fears torment, for she does not dare to tell her husband
that Col. James, smitten by her beauty, is now in pursuit of her.

In the opinion of L. H. Powers, Aeneas's descent into the
Underworld is echoed in *Amelia,* not in this equivalent Book VI,
but later in the Haymarket masquerade (Book X), where Miss
Matthews reappears reproachfully as Dido's phantom did. But
another writer on the subject, A. R. Towers, Jr., feels that Book I
of *Amelia,* with its striking account of condemned prisoners and

their punishments, brings to mind Virgil's depiction of the suffering souls encountered by Aeneas during his visit to Hades.[7]

BOOK VII

The whole of Book VII in *Amelia* is given over to the monologue of Mrs. Bennet (now Mrs. Atkinson), who intends her own
outlandish experiences with the Noble Lord to serve as a warning
for Amelia. After describing how the Trojan colonists landed at
the mouth of the Tiber and negotiated with King Latinus, this
book in the *Aeneid* turned away from the Trojans to tell at length
about the congregating of enemy warriors. If there is any striking
metaphorical parallel between these sections of the two works, it
is, as L. H. Powers phrases it, in Mrs. Bennet's providing arms,
through her testimony, to be wielded against the Noble Lord.
Mr. Powers not only identifies the Noble Lord with Turnus, who
defied Aeneas as a suitor for the hand of Lavinia, but identifies
Mrs. Bennet here with Venus, Aeneas's mother and protector.[8]
Mrs. Bennet loves to quote from the *Aeneid* in Latin and on
several occasions does so, though not always accurately.

BOOK VIII

Half the chapters in this book are spent with Booth among
other prisoners in the bailiff's charge, until Dr. Harrison finally
effects his release; the other chapters show Col. James's machin-
ations to possess Amelia. James is unwilling to assist her husband
unless she makes herself available to him. It is Mrs. Atkinson

---

[7] L. H. Powers, *op. cit.*, p. 331; A. R. Towers, Jr., " An Introduction and
Annotations for a Critical Edition of *Amelia*," unpubl. diss., Princeton Univ.
(1953), p. 116. See also R. W. Rader, " Idea and Structure in Fielding's
Novels," unpubl. diss., Indiana Univ. (1958), for the connection of Aeneas's
allegorical descent into Hell with initiation into the Eleusinian Mysteries
(pp. 385–387).

[8] L. H. Powers, *op. cit.*, p. 332.

who again sounds a warning to Amelia : "I believe the Person, who hath injured the Captain with this Friend of his, is one of the worthiest and best of Creatures—Nay, do not be surprised; the Person I mean is even your fair Self : Sure you would not be so dull in any other Case; but in this, Gratitude, Humility, Modesty, every Virtue, shuts your Eyes. *Mortales hebitant visus,* as Virgil says. What in the World can be more consistent, than his Desire to have you at his own House; and to keep your Husband confined in another?" There is a mustering of forces against both Col. James and the Noble Lord; for with Dr. Harrison reconciled, Booth freed from jail, and with the assistance of Sgt. Atkinson and his Latin-quoting wife, Amelia may keep her virtue victoriously. In the *Aeneid,* too, the action of Book VIII was that of suspenseful preparation for war, Aeneas being outfitted with armor by Venus, his mother.

BOOK IX

Action is intensified. A fight to protect Amelia seems unavoidable; and in a discussion of dueling, Col. Bath asks Dr. Harrison, "Nay, and in *Dryden's Virgil,* is there any Thing almost besides fighting?" Both Col. James and the Noble Lord renew their plans to assault Amelia's virtue, the Colonel attacking by a sly offer to pay Booth's debts and send him out of the country, his Lordship planning confidently when he meets Amelia in company with Mrs. James at a morning rout. In the *Aeneid* the Italian armies, led by Turnus, attacked Aeneas's camp at Ostia, representing the first major hostile action.

BOOK X

The first chapter here is mostly devoted to an amusing discussion, between Mrs. Atkinson and Dr. Harrison, of Virgil and the *Aeneid.* " You have heard," says Dr. Harrison, ". . . that *Virgil*

left his *Æneid* incorrect; and perhaps, had he lived to correct it,
we should not have seen the Faults we now see in it." Of all the
books in the *Aeneid*, this tenth one is considered most episodic,
unintegrated, and incomplete! The strongest parallels in Book X
occur at the Haymarket masquerade. Juno's passionate plea to
the other gods is not unlike Miss Matthews's "violent Upbraid-
ings" at the masquerade. Juno protected Turnus from death by
having him follow a harmless phantom in Aeneas's likeness, and
at the masquerade both the Noble Lord and Col. James pursue a
masked woman they believe is Amelia. The woman in the domino,
to whom his Lordship makes "very fervent Love" and to whom
the Col. whispers, is Mrs. Atkinson who indiscreetly encourages
his Lordship in hopes of assisting her own husband. The gods
were not yet reconciled to Venus's plans for Aeneas; and Booth,
though "an extreme well-wisher to Religion," is less reconciled to
Christianity than to his idea of "ruling passions." Amelia, who
suspects that he is "little better than an Atheist," assures him that
"there are really such Things as Religion and Virtue."

BOOK XI

Dr. Harrison tries unsuccessfully to procure recognition of
Booth's qualifications for advancement in the Army; but the
nobleman to whom he applies observes that it is not feasible "to
provide for all Men of Merit" (ch. ii). "At this point," George
Sherburn notices, "the two themes that Fielding uses in depict-
ing Booth's lot most nearly meet : his belief in a dominant passion
has sapped his zest for life as a moral struggle, and the lack of
recognition of his undisputed merit has destroyed incentive that
might lead him to excellence as a servant of his counry." Sherburn adds that Bossu, in his *Treatise of the Epick Poem* (Bk. I,
ch. xi, dealing with the *Aeneid*), provides an "analysis of epic
structure into a remotely similar dual motivation."[9]

---

[9] George Sherburn, *op. cit.*, p. 13n.

Distress felt by Aeneas at the death of Pallas may be echoed in that felt here by Amelia at the near-death of Sgt. Atkinson. The council of Italian princes to plot Aeneas's downfall may be echoed in the Noble Lord's plan, successful except in his desired end with Amelia, to be rid of Booth by having him imprisoned for a gambling debt; for when Amelia sells her possessions to repay the debt, Booth uses her money instead to try to buy Army preferment for himself. Col. James's challenge of Booth to a duel appears here, paralleling Turnus's agreement to meet Aeneas in a single combat. Poor Amelia opens James's letter to Booth asking for satisfaction the next morning at six ("I shall bring my Pistols with me"); almost immediately afterwards she receives her husband's apologetic letter from the bailiff's house. He has been apprehended upon leaving Miss Matthews who, again active in the plot, may be considered now as Camilla, the hostile *bellatrix* of the *Aeneid*.

BOOK XII

The duel with Col. James never occurs. Virgil had described how, after Turnus broke his agreement to gamble the terms of peace on his single combat with Aeneas, and battle raged, Aeneas finally faced his adversary to thrust a fatal sword into his breast. The gods were reconciled to the Trojans' destiny. In a complete reversal of the Booths' fortunes, Dr. Harrison persuades James to abandon his dueling challenge, James also abandons his plans for enjoying Amelia, and she suddenly learns that she is an heiress. Upon learning of her inheritance Amelia thanks Heaven and then embraces her husband; Mrs. Atkinson jumps about the room quoting from the *Aeneid*. But more significant, Booth in prison is converted to active Christianity and is reconciled to his God. By reading Barrow's sermons "in Proof of the Christian Religion," he has dropped all his doubts and is "reconciled to Truth at last." Like Aeneas, Booth ends his quest by coming into his own, not only by establishing his family, but by spiritual conversion, and reconciliation with the gods. Both Booth and Aeneas desire to start a new life : with their children the Booths at last establish themselves on their country estate near Salisbury; Aeneas and Lavinia established themselves in Latium.

"The *Aeneid*," says Northrop Frye, "develops the theme of return into one of rebirth"; and T. S. Eliot similarly remarks that "Aeneas' end is only a new beginning; and the whole point of the pilgrimage is something which will come to pass for future generations. . . . He is, in fact, the prototype of a Christian hero." [10] Amelia, to whom Fielding attributes "the Heroic Part of the female Character" (IX, ii), is a true Christian heroine. Although Booth becomes a kind of Christian hero through conversion, Fielding carefully avoids using "hero" as an epithet for him. Not the scoundrel and mere sensualist that Richardson was pleased to think him, Booth is — like Aeneas — occasionally foolish, acting on instinctive feelings, an agent committed to duties but lacking the strongest of inner convictions. Both are soldiers who feel no great joy in warfare : "The enemy is nominally Juno; more really it is inward weakness. Juno, Aeolus, Turnus, and others throw difficulties in the way, but the real fight is within." [11] Until his conversion this is even more true for Booth than for Aeneas.

Storied Aeneas, the son of a goddess, had his greatness as founder of the Roman nation sung in epic verse. Fielding's trans-

---

[10] Northrop Frye, *Anatomy of Criticism* (Princeton, 1957), p. 319; T. S. Eliot, " Virgil and the Christian World," *On Poetry and Poets* (New York, 1957), p. 143.

[11] T. R. Glover, *Virgil*, 6 ed. (London, 1930), p. 320. Glover writes that Aeneas " has not enough freedom of will. There are indeed such people to be met with in the world, but they rarely interest us " (p. 211). But to this rather captious comment Glover adds a footnote of reconsideration : " And yet after ten years more of life—I will not attempt autobiography, but Aeneas seems a more intelligible and sympathetic character." I think Booth may also become somewhat more intelligible and sympathetic as one's domestic involvements increase—not to attempt autobiography.

position causes Booth, the little officer on half-pay, to assume
some reflected, universal significance. Booth's characteristics, experiences, and fortunes take point from those of Virgil's hero,
lifting him above the absurd diminutiveness to be expected in
mock-heroic. Booth is ridiculous, but not in the way that Tom
Thumb, Mr. Booby, and Parson Trulliber are ridiculous.

Although E. M. W. Tillyard, in his study of the epic form as
it has disguised itself in English literature, comments somewhat
testily on *Tom Jones,* he says nothing of *Amelia,* which would
have offered him a more demonstrable example of imitation.[12]
In *Joseph Andrews* Fielding had announced his province as the
comic epic in prose; but in *Amelia,* as George Sherburn says,
"he follows, not the tradition of the comic epic—really that of
Cervantes and Scarron, among others—but rather a newer tradition of the epic in prose. The epic in prose, in its turn, is not so
much the tradition of *Telemachus* as it is a tradition of private
history done with fidelity to the facts of every-day life."[13] That is
almost to say, *Amelia* is a novel in the modern sense, like *Middle-
march, The Mayor of Casterbridge,* and *Ulysses.*

The eighteenth century, it is well known, considered the epic
to be the highest of literary forms, and fostered both burlesques
(presenting gods and heroes in "low" situations) and mock heroics
(with "low" persons aping the actions of gods and heroes). Following precedent, Fielding mimics the complete epic form in
Amelia, its twelve books dealing with national identity, voyages,
fights, a gauntlet of trials through which the hero must run, a
visit to the Underworld, harangues, intrigues, phantoms, and
supernatural machinery to arouse wonder in the reversal of
fortune at the end. In *The Rape of the Lock,* faithful to its
fashionable London setting, the supernatural machinery seems to
have taxed Pope's ingenuity considerably. His eventual, brilliant

---

[12] E. M. W. Tillyard, *The Epic Strain in the English Novel* (London,
1958), pp. 51–58.
[13] George Sherburn, *op. cit.,* p. 2.

addition of Rosicrucian sylphs and gnomes to provide epic "machinery" was not unlike Fielding's later use of the "ruling passions" which hover over the characters in *Amelia*.

Booth regards the passions as omnipresent forces or instincts which may carry a man's actions toward either useful or reprehensible ends. This "Doctrine of the Passions," he tells Miss Matthews, "had been his favourite Study" and "he was convinced every Man acted entirely from that Passion which was uppermost" (III, iv). All other elements of personality must be synthesized with the ruling passion, whichever it is, if a man is to live artfully. Although the theory had been dignified by its exposition in Montaigne's essays and in Pope's poems, it was— as Booth finally admits—a naive basis upon which to build an ethical system; for if only "passions spin the plot," a man's actions themselves cannot be considered either good or bad. Of Miss Matthews Booth says that "Vanity is plainly her predominant Passion" (IV, vi). He talks of the passion of honor, of hope, of fear, of pride, of friendship, of lust, of envy. "Love, Benevolence, or what you will please to call it" is the "reigning Passion" for Sgt. Atkinson (III, vii). But until Booth's rebirth or conversion, when at last he admits to the power of religion and virtue, even benevolence seems a mere Mandevillean gratification of self-love through "doing good, and by relieving the Distresses of others" (X, ix). Personal selfishness, a chameleon-like passion, he believes to be at the root of all social impulses, virtuous or vicious. But religious conversion dispels all the machinery of hovering passions whose "blind Guidance" hindered Booth's achievement of Christian happiness.

If I have dealt far more with Booth than with his wife Amelia, who gives her name to the title of the novel, it is, first, because she shares the fate of her namesake of a hundred years later, Amelia Sedley, who seems nobly insipid alongside the unscrupulous, complex, arresting Becky Sharp for whom she was intended to provide a contrast."[14] Fielding's Amelia, like Thackeray's, embodies patience and moral courage. She is, Fielding says in praise of her, "A Lady who was possessed of all the domestick Virtues of Life; and so remarkable for her Meekness of Disposition, as to have equalled the Fame of Patient *Grissel.*"[15] It is her wayward husband who allows her to seem interesting. And then I wonder whether Fielding did not intend both Amelia and Booth to appear glaringly incomplete and unsatisfactory when separated. This is the point of his epigraph *"Felices ter & amplius/Quos irrupta tenet Copula"* and of the proposition expressed in his first sentence, referring not to *arma virumque* but to "a very worthy Couple." Their union, threatened and tested throughout twelve books, is the announced theme of the novel. When Rebecca West remarks how Amelia, exemplifying the female redemptor snatching man from perdition, was to save Billy Booth "by harnessing his sensual nature to the sentiments of 'esteem and gratitude,' " she suggests their mutual need.[16] Perhaps, as I have earlier implied in the long outline of plot, Booth and Amelia joined must be considered the modern domestic equivalent of Virgil's hero if we bother to observe the novel's ironic correspondence with the *Aeneid.*

The ingenious Virgilian framework and overtones in *Amelia* are primarily amusing, it seems to me; but at the same time they serve to exalt the modern, "low," or familiar characters and situations. Although one of Fielding's motives was to expose injustices at hand—in the Army, Law, and Nobility especially—he was able, by wittily effecting an adjustment between the Trojan story and the modern situation, interpreting the *Aeneid* in local terms,

---

[14] See Sabine Nathan, "The Anticipation of Nineteenth Century Ideological Trends in Fielding's *Amelia,*" *Zeitschrift für Anglistik und Amerikanistik,* VI (1958), for an interpretation of Amelia as a heroine-in-spite-of-herself, without "insight enough," "too credulous," suffering from a "lack of perception," and "a dupe" (pp. 405, 406, 407).

[15] Henry Fielding, *The Covent-Garden Journal Extraordinary,* No. 1 (20 January, 1752).

[16] Rebecca West, *op. cit.,* p. 178.

to say again that human nature remains constant throughout history. Mimicry of Virgil's narrative serves perhaps as a laughing commentary on the epic form; but it also serves as a means to imply the epic heroism that may show itself in human nature around us. It contrasts "literature" and "life."

Because it has been generally unnoticed or unremarked upon, this interpretation (which can be called "symbolic," I suppose) has neither vexed nor delighted most readers of *Amelia*. Fielding has ordered his materials to allow the Virgilian original to show through but not to obtrude.

The seed from which the novel may have grown, as differentiated from its model, appears in two sentences from *Tom Jones*. In VII, xii, Tom joined the company of a lieutenant who had received no higher preferment in nearly forty years. Like Booth the lieutenant had been wounded in battle, was honest and good-natured, and was highly esteemed by his men. But the lieutenant's wife, like Amelia beautiful and faithful, had repulsed the amorous advances of her husband's colonel; and his career, like Booth's, suffered. Tom Jones's lieutenant "had the Misfortune to incur the Displeasure of his Colonel, who for many Years continued in the Command of this Regiment. Nor did he owe the implacable Ill-will which this Man bore him to any Neglect or Deficiency as an Officer, nor indeed to any Fault in himself; but solely to the Indiscretion of his Wife, who was a very beautiful Woman, and who, tho' she was remarkably fond of her Husband, would not purchase his Preferment at the Expence of certain Favours which the Colonel required of her." These two sentences from *Tom Jones* not only comprise much of the plot of *Amelia* in little, but are expressed through verbal irony more tautly stretched than almost anything that comes to mind in the later novel. The word "Indiscretion," in the sense of a transgression of social morality, is an ironic commentary on false social "systems" everywhere : it becomes the burden of thought in *Amelia*.

X

The Sermon at the Masquerade

Amelia

*The priest is preoccupied with thoughts of sin and the
redeeming effect of grace; the artist is busy portraying the
sinner and parodying the ways of grace. For parody is
his mode, as prayer is the mode proper to the priest.—
Kevin Sullivan.*[1]

One possible source for fiction as we know it may be found in
the medieval priests' *exempla,* moralized anecdotes to enliven and
illustrate the texts of sermons; and sermons have a way of creep-
ing ambiguously into modern fiction. I say "ambiguously"
because the reader is often aroused, edified, titillated, puzzled,
and entertained all at once. This is true, I think, even in the
Methodist sermon Dinah delivers under a tree to farmers in the
second chapter of *Adam Bede.* Minutely describing her, George
Eliot introduces Dinah as a self-consciously pretty woman performing dramatically before the country people who are at first
merely curious. The sermon is enthusiastically serious, but George
Eliot's projection of it flirts amusingly with parody.

Father Arnall's famous sermon in *A Portrait of the Artist as
a Young Man,* based upon *Hell Opened to Christians, To Caution
Them from Entering into It,* and upon the Jesuit *Sodality
Manual,* could be preached with high effect in another retreat;
but for James Joyce it may have been only an ironic device to

---

[1] Kevin Sullivan, *Joyce among the Jesuits* (New York, 1958), p. 145.

move Stephen Dedalus, who hears the sermon, toward his decision to become a creative artist.[2] Father Mapple's equally famous sermon in *Moby Dick* has been called "splendid rhetoric," "terrifying," "mock-serious," and "comic." It seems to be ironic preparation for the events that follow : "Father Mapple," says one critic, "is very serious, but Melville is the manipulator of this puppet show."[3]

Dr. Primrose, assiduously preaching to his fellow jail-birds "with a loud unaffected voice," at first inspires only merriment, lewd whispers, and "groans of contrition burlesqued"; but Goldsmith assures us that the Vicar is accorded breathless attention during his long sermon on the value of suffering—immediately after which there are discoveries, recognitions, and reversals of the Vicar's fortunes. The sermon is a different thing depending upon whether you read it as melodrama, satire, homily, or mere plot-device.[4] Much funnier is Dr. Slop's sermon which is read out by Corporal Trim, with a false start, interruptions, objections, interpolations, and arguments in Book II of *Tristram Shandy;* but this sermon, Sterne's own, had been preached by him in the cathedral at York and had already been published. Sterne's "topics of rhetoric become less important than the psychological fact that rhetoric becomes a topic of rhetoric; the reader becomes his own foil."[5]

Henry Fielding cannot be said to have invented this device of the ambiguous sermon (it can be seen in Richardson's fiction too), but he is the earliest novelist to use it consistently and importantly. His three "father-figures," Parson Adams, Squire Allworthy, and

---

[2] *Ibid.,* pp. 138 ff., and James R. Thrane, " Joyce's Sermon on Hell : Its Source and Its Background," *Modern Philology,* LVII (February, 1960), 172–198.

[3] Lawrance Thompson, *Melville's Quarrel with God* (Princeton, 1952), p. 164.

[4] See F. W. Hilles, Introduction, *The Vicar of Wakefield,* Everyman's Library American Ed. (New York, 1951), ix–xv.

[5] John Traugott, *Tristram Shandy's World: Sterne's Philosophical Rhetoric* (Berkeley and Los Angeles, 1954), p. 83.

Dr. Harrison, who finally relinquish their authority to Joseph Andrews, Tom Jones, and the Booths, are likely to sermonize on almost any occasion, even against protests. Fielding does not burlesque or subvert their moral or philosophical assumptions; he does, however, show the sermons to be inappropriate to the situation, inconsistent with the speaker's own actions, or open to misinterpretation. The sermons are often ironic preparations for ensuing developments in characterization, theme, and story.

With irreverent comments and interruptions Dr. Harrison's sermon on adultery in *Amelia* is read out at the Haymarket Opera-house (X, ii). The occasion is a masquerade attended by Col. James and his wife, Col. Bath, Miss Matthews, the Noble Lord, Booth, and Mrs. Atkinson. All are of course in disguise, and by wearing Amelia's domino Mrs. Atkinson is mistaken for her by everyone including Booth himself. Miss Matthews, frustrated in her wishes to resume an adulterous relationship with Booth, treats him reproachfully. Col. James, who has invited Amelia to the masquerade in hopes of establishing an adulterous relationship with her, is frustrated because Mrs. Atkinson, whom he takes to be Amelia, spends her evening in conversation with the lust-sick Noble Lord. Impersonating Amelia, Mrs. Atkinson hints broadly to the Noble Lord that an adulterous relationship depends only upon securing a captaincy for Sgt. Atkinson.

Knowing of Col. James's designs upon Amelia's virtue, Dr. Harrison has sent him an unsigned sermon-letter appealing to his reason, decency, and fear of God. Even if adultery had "not been so expressly forbidden in Scripture," he writes, "still the Law of Nature would have yielded Light enough for us to have discovered the great Horror and Atrociousness of this Crime. . . . And sure in a human Sense there is scarce any Guilt which deserves to be more severely punished.

*   *   *

" Domestic Happiness is the End of almost all our Pursuits, and the common Reward of all our Pains. When Men find themselves

for ever barred from this delightful Fruition, they are lost to all
Industry, and grow careless of all their worldly Affairs. Thus they
become bad Subjects, bad Relations, bad Friends and bad Men.
Hatred and Revenge are the wretched Passions which boil in their
Minds. Despair and Madness very commonly ensue, and Murder
and Suicide often close the dreadful Scene.

"You are attacking a Fortress on a Rock; a Chastity so strongly
defended, as well by a happy natural Disposition of Mind as by the
strongest Principles of Religion and Virtue, implanted by Education
and nourished and improved by Habit, that the Woman must be
invincible even without that firm and constant Affection of her
Husband, which would guard a much looser and worse-disposed
Heart.

                            *   *   *

"I can think of but one Argument more, and that indeed a very
bad one : You throw away that Time in an impossible Attempt,
which might, in other Places, crown your sinful Endeavours with
Success."

There are eleven paragraphs in all, in Col. James's opinion
"a very impertinent Letter, something like a Sermon, against
Adultery" (XII, iv). When the Colonel loses it out of his pocket
at the masquerade, it is picked up by an "Assembly of young
Fellows, whom they call Bucks" and is mockingly declaimed by
one of their number for the general amusement. One of the bucks
suggests having the sermon set to music by Handel for an oratorio.
"' D––n me, *Jack,*' says another, 'we'll have it set to a Psalm
Tune, and we'll sing it next *Sunday* at St. *James*'s Church, and
I'll bear a Bob, d––n me' " (X, ii).

Their horseplay is interrupted by Col. Bath, masquerading as a
friar, whose "tremendous Majesty" and threat of violence in the
name of religion and virtue send the mockers flying. The sermon-
letter is left in his hands. He reads it and, making "many Enco-
miums upon it," passes it along to Booth, in whose pocket it
remains during his long dialogue with Miss Matthews, who is

masquerading as a shepherdess. It is not until the next morning and after happily learning that Amelia was not at the Haymarket with him after all, that Booth finds the letter in his pocket and reads it with curiosity and interest. He recognizes Dr. Harrison's handwriting (X, iv). When Booth that morning shows Dr. Harrison the sermon-letter and says he received it from "a noble Colonel" at the Haymarket, the good Doctor is astounded, for he believes Booth to mean Col. James himself. Joining the two men, Mrs. Atkinson now remarks that at the masquerade "there was a young Fellow that had preached a Sermon there upon a Stool, in Praise of Adultery, she believed." Her misconception and the preposterous idea of Col. Bath (known to his subordinate officers as "Old Honour and Dignity") as Amelia's would-be lover throw Booth into a fit of laughter; and Dr. Harrison, who thinks his sermon is the source of Booth's amusement, is offended (X, iv).

And Fielding has not yet finished with his uses for the sermon-letter. That afternoon while walking in the Park, Booth meets Col. Bath, who asks for its return. Booth gives it to him but remarks that the Colonel seems to him an unlikely recipient of such an anonymous warning. The Colonel is indignant, saying that he took it "from a Set of idle young Rascals, one of whom was reading it out aloud upon a Stool, while the rest were attempting to make a Jest, not only of the Letter, but of all Decency, Virtue, and Religion" (X, v). Now Booth suspects the truth, that "he had mistaken one Colonel for another," and that Col. Bath's brother-in-law, Col. James, was the man to whom the sermon-letter had been addressed by Dr. Harrison. Booth asks to have it back in his possession and returns it to his pocket. He intends to confront Col. James by reading it aloud to him and watching his reaction; and after quelling his husbandly suspicions of Amelia he relates "all the Circumstances of the Letter" to her (X, vi).

Col. James has now sent a message challenging Booth to a duel on account of Miss Matthews, and Dr. Harrison calls on him to try to intercede (XII, iv). At this meeting Dr. Harrison learns that it was not Colonel James but his brother-in-law who gave the sermon-letter to Booth at the masquerade. When James is mildly threatening to Dr. Harrison, he says—in effect now concluding his sermon on adultery: "You tell me, Sir, . . that my Gown is my Protection; let it then at least protect me where I have had no Design in offending; where I have consulted your highest Welfare, as in truth I did in writing this Letter. And if you did not in the least deserve any such Suspicion, still you have no Cause for Resentment. Caution against Sin, even to the Innocent, can never be unwholesome."

Clearly, by the time he wrote *Amelia* there had been no diminishing of Fielding's genius in the invention and management of incidents, the minute wheels, "almost imperceptible," which set the great wheels of the world in motion. The incident of the sermon on adultery read out by a buck at the masquerade, entertaining in itself, is attended by a series of intricacies and complications, each of them naturally evolving and consistent with the "truth" of the fictional world in *Amelia,* and leading the imagination of the reader through some ingeniously varied revelations and reversals towards a conclusion that should be judicious, inevitable, and amusingly satisfying. Nothing in *Tom Jones,* famous (or infamous) for its constructive art, out-does Fielding's show of "architectonics" in developing the incident of Dr. Harrison's sermon-letter.

Like the fictional sermons of Dr. Slop, Father Mapple, and Father Arnall, which followed this one in three different centuries, Dr. Harrison's is somewhat ambiguous in its presentation. It is funny in its rakish, almost raffish setting. The irreverent and bawdy comments of the young bucks are entertaining in the fashion of the obscene legal jokes applied to Joseph Andrews when he rode naked in the coach after his roadside beating. The scene at the Opera-house, with a company of persons disguised in costumes, dominoes, and masks, is amusingly appropriate to a sermon on adultery—an activity usually involving pretense, deceit, and masquerade; and all the characters present who are important to the novel are involved, the reader already knows, in one way or another with adultery. When Mrs. Atkinson, whose faculties were too much engaged in hinting at adultery with the Noble Lord to hear the sermon correctly, says that she believes it to have been in *favor* of adultery, the reader cannot help joining Booth in laughter.

But the sermon withstands the test of laughter and ridicule. It seems least serious, perhaps, in its final argument, that Col. James could less troublesomely cap his "sinful Endeavours with Success" elsewhere than with Amelia; but there Dr. Harrison seems to want to shock James into awareness of his situation. Shock is the preacher's last resort.

Otherwise, Dr. Harrison's animadversions on adultery might be Fielding's own as he expressed his opinions elsewhere in print. In his "Charge to the Grand Jury" (1749), delivered as magistrate for Westminster and chairman of the Quarter Sessions of the Peace, he included among other crimes and offenses those of fornication and adultery, though pointing out that they had mostly been given over to ecclesiastical jurisdiction. In *Amelia* itself he has Dr. Harrison inquire : "In the great Sin of Adultery for Instance; hath the Government provided any Law to punish it? or doth the Priest take any Care to correct it? On the contrary, is the most notorious Practice of it any Detriment to a Man's Fortune or to his Reputation in the World? Doth it exclude him from any Preferment in the State, I had almost said in the Church? Is it any Blot in his Escutcheon? Any Bar to his Honour? Is he not to be found every Day in the Assemblies of Women of the highest Quality? In the Closets of the greatest Men, and even at the Tables of Bishops? (IX, v). Following the publication of *Amelia,* in three issues of *The Covent-Garden Journal* Fielding continues with the subject, introducing it in No. 66, for 14 October, 1752, and making it the entire subject in Nos. 67 and 68, for 21 and 28 October. He questions "whether Adultery be really that Matter of Jest and Fun which it is conceived to be" and, turning to comparative anthropology of an amateur sort, cites how adultery has been punished in various times and places—in Rome, Egypt, China, parts of Guinea, Arabia, Fida, and Patane, with javelin-piercing, boiling water, castration, and death as examples (No. 67); and then he cites laws against adultery (No. 68).

For both the imaginary Dr. Harrison and Fielding the magistrate and moralist, the sermon at the masquerade was a serious exhortation directed at the private and the public conscience. For Fielding the novelist, the sermon at the masquerade is also an amusing incident, an ingenious device, and a manifestation of the constructive power of his genius. It is the feigning of a moral masquerade.

It shows the deepening stream of the subject matter that interested him as his facility with fiction allowed him to plunge further into problems of human nature. After the reversal of moral values in *Shamela*, as parody demands, he dealt with continence in *Joseph Andrews*, incontinence in *Tom Jones*, and now adultery in *Amelia*. His point of view was always that of the male, conceiving the heroines as beautiful, patient, scrupulously virtuous refuges, though constantly tempted and tried, to whom Joseph, Tom, and Booth unquestioningly commit themselves. But his point of view is also that of the judge who must distinguish between the seriousness of one crime and another. Joseph's long-suffering chastity and the sexual defections of Tom and Booth contrast with the social injustices, public cruelties, hypocrisies, unbridled lusts, and cancerous hatreds that make up a large part of the background for Fielding's comic works of fiction.[6]

---

[6] " *Amelia*, like *Tom Jones*, deals with wider issues than the modification of character. It has to do not merely with Booth and his wife, but with miseries and distresses typical of mid-eighteenth century London life. No other novel provides such a wide panorama of London society or better conveys what it was like to live in London in the seventeen-fifties."—John Butt, *Fielding*, Writers and Their Work Bibliographical Series, No. 57 (London, 1954), p. 27.

XI

The Art of Life

Amelia

*By examining carefully the several Gradations which
conduce to bring every Model to Perfection, we learn
truly to know that Science in which the Model is formed:
As Histories of this Kind, therefore, may properly be
called Models of Human Life; so by observing minutely
the several Incidents which tend to the Catastrophe or
Completion of the whole, and the minute Causes whence
those Incidents are produced, we shall best be instructed
in this most useful of all Arts, which I call the Art of
Life. — Amelia, I, i.*

In the preceding essays I have tried to keep my eye on works of
literature as such and have sought no golden key to unlock the
secret cabinets of Henry Fielding's rugged heart. Because he is
remembered for his published fiction, Fielding's works are his
true and significant biography. Many other magistrates have
given charges to grand juries; many other widowers have married
their dead wives' maids; many others have died of dropsy, perhaps even in Lisbon; but no one else wrote *Tom Jones* and
Amelia.

The art of fiction in relation to life is usually, I think, treated
in one of three general ways. One of these approaches will try
to enforce the idea of life modeled upon art or revealed only
through art — by means of a severe selection, rearrangement, and

redesigning of the materials we associate with life, to create a pattern audaciously unfamiliar, aesthetically demanding, and — if it succeeds — more "true" to life than the less radical approaches. *Tristram Shandy, The Sacred Fount,* and *Ulysses* represent this kind, though the tantalizing dream of a novel about nothing at all except its own style, sustained by its sheer brilliance rather than by any kind of representation, would be an example more nearly perfect. A second approach is to think of fiction as an illumination of the shadowy experience we call life, the throwing here and there of a tenuous shaft of light to make clear for a moment some relationship, some insight, or some meaning that has been only dimly discerned — as in portions of *Clarissa* and all of *Nightwood.* The other, older way is to look upon the novel as a mirrored reflection of life, in which the cold pane of silvered glass is held up to show within the limits of its frame the noon-time glare, the plate of hashed mutton, the blue domino at the masquerade, the nervous gestures, lingering embraces, and crooked smiles of the "real" world as we imagine we know it. Here is *Mansfield Park* as well as *Moll Flanders.*

Most of Fielding's fiction, pretty certainly, is in the category of "mirrored reflection of life," courting recognition in the reader for its most telling effects. More than is generally admitted there is too — as this book tries to show — a good deal of "illumination of what is shadowy" in his fiction; for although he is properly identified with manly openness, sunlight, and fresh air, he repeatedly demonstrated that he was interested in probing into unsuspected motives, drawing fine moral distinctions in his appraisals of human nature. Artfully distilling and taking from life as he experienced or observed it, ordering his materials to conduct his readers into a world of imagined reality more real than the real one, Fielding had much to say on what he thought truly valuable in life. As the art of fiction must be drawn from life, the art of life might be based reciprocally, he thought, upon fictional representations.

The comic humanism of *Joseph Andrews* and *Tom Jones* presumes that the vagaries of human nature can be made to submit to the test of reason. Even the most sympathetic characters, like Parson Adams, when they deviate beyond the boundaries of reason, are laughable. But the same comic humanism denies that human nature and reason are wholly compatible. One's sympathy is with Joseph Andrews's *un*reasonableness when he and Parson Adams are tied to the bedpost; and Tom Jones's healthy good nature when joined by prudence takes ascendance over Squire Allworthy's benign but sometimes mistaken reason. Fielding's comic understanding of human nature and the exterior world was one of tolerance; and in the prefaces to *Tom Jones* he argued for sympathetic involvement and against prejudicial responses.

Tolerance, however, as V. S. Pritchett remarks in connection with Fielding, may induce "a blunting of the powers of moral discrimination," by which I suppose he means that the logical end of tolerance is indifference. But Mr. Pritchett goes on to say that "one has only to consider Fielding's attitude to sexual love to see that his tolerance was based on intelligent sympathy and curiosity and, what is most important to comedy, on the power of making psychological distinctions. . . . He does not hate sexual love because he does not hate life. His good women are as emotionally disturbing as the bad ones. This is a generous compliment to virtue."[1] In a like manner Fielding amusingly and shrewdly made distinctions with "intelligent sympathy and curiosity" concerning most other experiences of life both private and public. In this respect *Joseph Andrews* and *Tom Jones* may, for the reader who observes "the several Incidents which tend to the Catastrophe or Completion of the Whole," offer worth-while instruction in the art of life.

Instruction in *Amelia* is colored by a more insistent mood. I have tried to show in the two preceding essays that Fielding's

---

[1] V. S. Pritchett, " The Tough School," *The Listener,* LI (20 May, 1954), 862.

power of brilliant elaboration, eye for the ridiculous, and tight-rope mastery of style are not lacking in *Amelia;* the comic sensi-bility lingers. But here Fielding is more overtly the "Christian Censor," the Pelagian adherent of latitudinarian benevolism, and the dramatizer of homilies preached by divines like Barrow, South, Tillotson, and Clarke. Although its action opens "On the first of *April,* in the Year – – – –," *Amelia* is no April Fool's jest except in the most general, cosmic sense.

George Saintsbury pointed out that barely three years' time elapsed between the publishing of *Tom Jones* and of *Amelia,* so that Fielding may have worked on them almost consecutively.[2] But a "pre-Victorian" atmosphere in *Amelia* has dissuaded some readers from enjoying the Augustan irony and raciness of style it shares with *Tom Jones.* Its relationship to *Joseph Andrews,* of ten years earlier, is almost precisely that of Jane Austen's ironic "pre-Victorian" *Mansfield Park* to one of her earliest master-pieces of comic irony, *Northanger Abbey.*

Except for I, i, the introductory essays are missing from *Amelia.* When Fielding uses his prerogative as "author" to interpolate pithy aphorisms, they are likely to be plainly stated in *Amelia,* unlike the waggish, mock-grandiose, or intentionally hackneyed commentaries that frequently appear in the earlier works. Field-ing now writes, for instance, regarding human conduct or the art of life :

In fact, if we regard this World only, it is the Interest of every Man to be either perfectly good or completely bad. He had better destroy his Conscience than gently wound it. The many bitter Reflections which every bad Action costs a Mind in which there are any Remains of Goodness are not to be compensated by the highest Pleasures which such an Action can produce. (IV, ii)

*   *   *

Ambition scarce ever produces any Evil but when it reigns in

[2] George Saintsbury, "Fielding," *Prefaces and Essays* (London, 1933), p. 52.

cruel and savage Bosoms; and Avarice seldom flourishes at all but
in the basest and poorest Soil. Love, on the contrary, sprouts
usually up in the richest and noblest Minds; but there, unless nicely
watched, pruned, and cultivated, and carefully kept clear of those
vicious Weeds which are too apt to surround it, it branches forth
into Wildness and Disorder, produces nothing desirable, but choaks
up and kills whatever is good and noble in the Mind where it so
abounds. (VI, i)

* * *

Indeed, Fear is never more uneasy than when it doth not certainly know its Objects; for on such Occasions the Mind is ever
employed in raising a thousand Bugbears and Fantoms, much more
dreadful than any Realities, and, like Children when they tell tales
of Hobgoblins, seems industrious in terrifying itself. (VI, iv)

* * *

Few Men, I believe, think better of others than of themselves;
nor do they easily allow the Existence of any Virtue of which they
perceive no Traces in their own Minds; for which Reason I have
observed, that it is extremely difficult to persuade a Rogue that you
are an Honest Man; nor would you ever succeed in the Attempt
by the strongest Evidence, was it not for the comfortable Conclusion
which the Rogue draws, that he who proves himself to be honest
proves himself to be a Fool at the same Time. (VI, viii)

* * *

The Truth is, that it is almost impossible Guilt should miss the
discovering of all the Snares in its Way, as it is constantly prying
closely into every Corner in order to lay Snares for Others. Whereas
Innocence, having no such Purpose, walks fearlessly and carelessly
through Life, and is consequently liable to tread on the Gins which
Cunning hath laid to entrap it. (VIII, ix)

These five moral observations—on Goodness, Love, Fear,
Opinions of Others, and Innocence—are mildly witty, mildly
cynical, perceptive, and aphoristically sound. The style is author-
itative, unhurried, and "plain," although Love is presented in
terms of gardening and Innocence is allegorized as walking

amongst snares and traps. Although these five quotations, like numbers of others in *Amelia,* need no context and could be printed in a *Collection of Moral and Instructive Sentiments, Maxims, Cautions, and Reflections* like the one Samuel Richardson culled from his own novels, all five have their jobs to perform in the fabric of the novel; they prepare the reader or summarize for him, they ask for reconsideration of the actions of characters, and two or three of them foreshadow incidents that lie ahead in the imaginary world of *Amelia.* All five can be utilized in perfecting the art of life.

There are other differences in *Amelia.* W. B. Coley lists three "modal changes" in the work, the first of these being a reduction in the "deliberate ironic discrepancy between the assumed identities ('author' and 'reader') and their implied, 'real' counterparts (Fielding and his audience)." That seems to me to be true. I am less convinced by Mr. Coley's second "modal change," of "emphasis on Prudence rather than on Fortune as the guiding principle of the action"; for as I have tried to show in "Some Minute Wheels," Prudence is a controlling theme in *Tom Jones*; and Amelia's becoming an heiress has no more connection with Booth's gaining Prudence than the discovery of Tom's parentage has with his gaining that same virtue. The other "modal change" deals with an altered conception of the theme I have made central in examining Fielding's fiction, that of "the relationship between literature and life." In *Amelia,* says Mr. Coley, we are no longer offered "world-stage analogies involving harlequinades or the farcical stuffing of coincidence and reversal. . . . Instead, life is to be envisioned through the spectacle of books, through a poetics, so to speak."[3]

In *Tom Jones,* as we have seen in connection with the device of Sophia Western's muff, Fielding drew attention to little incidents "which are very minute, and almost imperceptible to any

---

[3] W. B. Coley, "The Background of Fielding's Laughter," *ELH,* XXVI (June, 1959), 249–252.

but the strongest Eyes," but which move the "great Wheels" of fiction and of the world-machine. There his emphasis was upon instructing the reader in what to look for in fiction, especially in the new form of the comic novel that he was perfecting. But in *Amelia* he seems predominantly to want to instruct the reader in living : "so by observing minutely the several Incidents which tend to the Catastrophe or Completion of the whole, and the minute Causes whence those Incidents are produced, we shall best be instructed in this most useful of all Arts, which I call the Art of Life." In *Amelia* the "world-stage" analogy prevails, but the performance to be watched is a rehearsal for life itself in the married state.

Shamela (1741) is fiction laughing at fiction through parody and is only rudely like the world as we think we know it. *Joseph Andrews* (1742) moves from burlesque towards conviction of "reality." *Tom Jones* (1749), instructing its reader how fiction should be conceived and experienced, evokes a controlled, recognizable world within its pages — a world in which the sympathetic reader finds himself involved. In *Amelia* (1751), however, fiction is proffered as a preparation and guide for one's conduct in the real world, turning from bookishness to life itself. By borrowing its structure from the *Aeneid,* Fielding in *Amelia* interprets life in terms of literature as well as interpreting literature in terms of life.

Important in all the fiction, deepening or shifting in emphasis along the way, are three or four continuing themes. One of these depicts man's uncertainty as to whether Prudence or Fortune bestows the saving grace. Another theme deals with human nature's "glaring" qualities, from which even heroes and heroines are not exempt. A third is that of ecclesiastical, civil, and sexual corruptions and hypocrisies; with the latter is associated the theme of a "bad" woman's corrupting power, contrasted with the redeeming power of a "good" woman.

To render these themes and others, Henry Fielding juxtaposed or superimposed literature and life, showing the relationships of imagination and experience, puppets and people, myth and reality, stage and bed, Biblical Abraham and Abraham Adams, Hamlet's ghost and Tom Jones's ghost, the structure of the *Aeneid* and the structure of *Amelia,* the Haymarket masquerade and moral masquerades: the art of fiction and the art of life. The relationship of literature and life is itself one of his most constant themes. If we believe — with Fielding — that fiction can assist us in mastering reality, that theme should be of significance to us.

Some Dates

1707 (April 22) Henry Fielding born, probably at Sharpham Park, near Glastonbury, in Somersetshire. His boyhood was spent at East Stour, in Dorsetshire.

1719 Enrolled at Eton.

1724 Left Eton.

1728 " Love in Several Masques : A Comedy. "

1728–1729 At University of Leyden.

1730 " The Temple Beau : A Comedy "; " The Author's Farce "; "Tom Thumb : A Tragedy"; "Rape upon Rape : A Comedy."

1731 " The Letter-Writers : A Farce"; " The Welsh Opera."

1732 " The Lottery : A Farce "; " The Modern Husband : A Comedy"; "The Old Debauchess : A Comedy" "The Covent-Garden Tragedy "; " The Mock Doctor : A Comedy, Done from Molière."

1733 " The Miser : A Comedy, Taken from Plautus and Molière."

1734 Married to Charlotte Cradock. " The Intriguing Chamber-maid : A Comedy "; " Don Quixote in England : A Comedy."

1735 " An Old Man Taught Wisdom : A Farce "; " The Universal Gallant : A Comedy."

1736 Birth of Charlotte Fielding (d. 1742). " Pasquin : A Dramatick Satire on the Times"; "Tumble-Down Dick : A Dramatick Entertainment."

1737 Birth of Harriot Fielding (d. 1766). Theatrical Licensing Act. Entered as law student at the Middle Temple. " Eurydice : A Farce "; " The Historical Register for the Year 1736."

1739 (November 15)–1741 (June) Editor of " The Champion."

1740 Called to Bar and practised on the Western Circuit.

1741 (April 4) *An Apology for the Life of Mrs. Shamela Andrews. In which, the many notorious Falshoods and Misrepr[e]senta-*

tions of a Book called PAMELA, Are exposed and refuted; and all the matchless Arts of that young Politician, set in a true and just Light. Together with A full Account of all that passed between her and Parson Arthur Williams; whose Character is represented in a manner something different from what he bears in PAMELA. The whole being exact Copies of authentick Papers delivered to the Editor.

1742 (February 22) *The History of the Adventures of Joseph Andrews and of his friend, Mr. Abraham Adams. Written in Imitation of the Manner of Cervantes, Author of DON QUIXOTE* (2 vols.).

1743 " Miscellanies " (3 vols., including " A Journey from this World to the Next "; " The Life of Mr. Jonathan Wild the Great "; and " The Wedding-Day : A Comedy ").

1744 Death of Mrs. Fielding. Preface to 2nd ed. of Sarah Fielding's " Adventures of David Simple."

1745 (November 5) — 1746 (June 17) Editor of " The True Patriot."

1746 " The Female Husband."

1747 Married to Mary Daniell. Preface and contributions to Sarah Fielding's " Letters between the Principal Characters of David Simple, and Some Others."

1747 (December 5) — 1748 (November 5). Editor of " The Jacobite's Journal."

1748 Birth of William Fielding (d. 1820); birth of Mary Amelia Fielding (d. 1749). Appointed police-court magistrate at Bow Street; commissioned justice of the peace for Westminster.

1749 (February 28) *The History of Tom Jones, A Foundling* (6 vols.).

1749 " A Charge delivered to the Grand Jury "; " A True State of the Case of Bosavern Penlez." Jurisdiction as magistrate extended to entire county of Middlesex.

1750 Birth of Sophia Fielding (d. before 1757).

1751 (December 18) *Amelia* (4 vols.).

1751 "An Enquiry into the Causes of the late Increase of Robbers."

1752 Birth of Louisa Fielding (d. 1753).

1752 (January 4–November 25) Editor of " The Covent-Garden Journal."

1753 " A Proposal for Making an Effectual Provision for the Poor"; " A Clear State of the Case of Elizabeth Canning."

1754 Birth of Allen Fielding (d. 1823). Rev. ed. of " The Life of Mr. Jonathan Wild the Great."

1754 (October 8). Death of Henry Fielding in Lisbon, where he was buried.

1755 " The Journal of a Voyage to Lisbon."

Index